HELPLESSNESS

HELPLESSNESS

Dr. Shiv Mohan Mishra

GenNext Publication

ISBN : 978-93-8022-252-3
Price : ₹ 280

First Published, 2015

Published by,

genNext Publication
23, Main Ansari Road, Darya Ganj
New Delhi-110002
Ph. : 23242060, 23261060
Fax : 011-23285914
E-mail: gennext@hotmail.com
Website : www.gyanbooks.com

Laser Typesetting : Rajender Vashist, Delhi.
Printed at : G. Print Process, Delhi.

Cataloging in Publication Data—DK
Courtesy: D.K. Agencies (P) Ltd. <docinfo@dkagencies.com>

Mishra, Shiv Mohan, author.
Helplessness / Dr. Shiv Mohan Mishra. — First edition.
pages cm
Novel.
ISBN 9789380222523

1. Indic fiction (English). I. Title.

DDC 823.92 23

Dedication

This is my first work as a fiction to which I dedicate on the feet of my gracious and divinely gentle mother to whom I called 'Mata Ji' Late Mrs. Maha Laxmi Mishra who is the chief nourisher of my life and the most powerful source of my all sorts of knowledge and wisdom.

Simultaneosly the book is also dedicated to my worthy, gallant and heroic patron i.e., my father, Late Pandit Seeta Ram Mishra who has taught me the lessons of hard labour, sincere industry and good work very carefully. Without mentioning his name, it will be a quite incomplete assertion of my gratitudefulness.

Contents

Preface

Our country India has a very glorious record of human relations of the past. Perhaps India is the only country where passions, sentiments and emotions are valued greater than any other country of the world. Though human life is full of unaccountable sorts of relations but the relation between a man and a woman is the prime and the most important subject of all the most important literary works all over the world. Among the abundance of man-woman relations few relations are so impressive, praise worthy, critical and sometime so bitter that they force the genius to think and to say something about them. The novel 'Helplessness' contains a very hazardous and heart rendering relation of a mouth bursting wench like wife and a very serene, blessed, innocent and humble husband in a very queer manner. The description of the universal power of the love in the novel is the most praiseworthy aspect of the work.

Acknowledgements

Modern time is full of hurry, worry, unnumbered maladies and divided aims. It is the time of mental chaos, spiritual bankruptcy, noise, confusion and dominating materialism. In this world of hollow, wooden and mechanical people, I am not any exception rather I am also the busiest creature of business. The persons who inspired, co-operated and provided me a chance to write this novel are most unforgettable. So I enumerate their names one by one with the deep sense of gratitude. First of all I feel much grateful to my wife Mrs. Dharam Sheela Mishra who is the biggest source of inspiration for this work. She is also the strong cause of stimulation behind this fiction. I acknowledge a lot of gratitude for my one office assistant who always supported me in the moments of my emotional thoughtfulness. I pay my heartful thanks to Mr. Tarik Iqbal, Madam Gausiya Kausar and the most co-operative one, Mr. Ved Prakash Sharma who have given their precious times in the accomplishment of this task.

PART–I

1

A Sabrejet Unto the Heart

"After all you came, O mongrel! A bastard, meaner than a dirty cur. Has Sona, the foul widow quit you? Where hast thou been? Were you busy with that leprous bitch in taking the lustful joy of hers putting your head into her lap and smelling her foul and dirty body organs, lout, mean, worse than senseless. O wild Brute! Are you giving this very guidance to your sons and daughters? You call yourself as a teacher, hell on you what a rubbish boor and uncouth man you are. You must drown into a handful of water, such persons do not have a right to stay alive. You don't feel any shame in playing such licentious act with such a mean woman, perhaps belly is empty now, glut it with the whole food of the house, came the devil the glutton unfortunate, so many people die in accidents and road mishaps but nothing happens with this *Satan* remember "the mean" when you will die even the rotten dog of the street will not drop its urine on your face. Depraved insect of the gutter, 1you shall die any or other day, certainly you will surely meet a worse end"Anala showered such abusing hateful epithets on Dr. Nilay as soon as he put his first foot on the main gate of his large house.

These abuses and curses did not make any impression upon

Dr. Nilay, as he was accustomed to be shocked. It was the daily welcome of Nilay's teenager, married wife Anala, who possessed good qualities of womanhood and woman garniture except good behaviour whose soul victim was Dr. Nilay. Anala was a beautiful woman of thirty-eight years of age. She had a very fair complexion. Her hands and feet were so tender, smart and beautiful that none can accept the fact that such woman can also behave like beast. She possessed very fair middling body stature, curly hair, dimpled cheeks, beautiful chin, and long smooth ivory neck. When she wept, she looked as innocent and pious, which was enough to mislead even a wise judge. Anala was a very sharp-tongued woman, who opened her mouth for nothing, but to offend and abuse Nilay.

Having heard and received Anala's severe welcome, Dr. Nilay Sir only made a tragic smile on his psychological face and entered in to his only room with bent head. She chased behind with same tone.

"Have you gorged your sexual instincts much today? Was the swine not ready to leave you? Fear from God, O cur! every body is spitting at your name. It is very difficult to live in this *mohalla* now. The people all the time talk vulgarly about this pig. Even your children are talking obscenely about you. They don't like to be called themselves your children.

Continuing in the same tone, Anala threw the food before 'Nilay sir' and gave no pause to her tongue in giving injuries after injuries to him. Dr. Nilay a worthy, substantial, potential, learned and a quiet healthy man of thirty-five years old, would listen to her abuses with patience. He was helpless and forced to listen. There was no end or stop of Anala's heart rendering incestuously blameful words. Bearing every thing like rapt Lord Buddha, he patiently tolerated her ill-words for a long time. But, sometimes, he would also lose control upon himself and began to abuse Anala like an uncouth brute and crossed all the limits of saying. He appeared very mean person then whoever heard his dirty words and abuses marked Nilay sir as a wilder.......

2

Dr. Nilay's Fortitude and Liberality

The soul tormenting behaviour of Analawati Devi was enough to instigate a piece loving *yogi*. Generally, people do not like to take food in such circumstance, when any man's stubborn and wicked wife so hatefully serves it but the matter was entirely different and critical with Nilay sir. Though, his soul continued weeping, his psyche remained panting, nevertheless he had to take food. It was his helplessness. The meal of hotel and restaurants did not suit him. Often his appetite, got badly dismayed. He had the empire of very vast responsibilities to hold which he could not ignore. He had to handle, direct and investigate three Management and Technology colleges of which he was a sole owner, the founder and the chief managing director. None, but I alone know how hard and prolonged labour has provided these authorities to Nilay sir. I have been working in his institution for last eighteen years. I have seen the most earlier days, his primary beginning, his hard emergence when he came from distant village after being ruined in flood and cutting of the disastrous river Ghaghra, the border of the district Geetapur. He brought one pair of paint, shirt and an old cycle out of his parental properties, for twenty years he sacrificed all sorts of pleasures and embraced sufferings, starvation, poverty etc. He spent many sleepless nights, but did not surrender before situations. He went on fighting with buffets and storms of life. I am the eye witness of these sufferings. Often, I began to think whether another Christ asçended on earth for the sake of humanity, because none but I know about his love for the poor, helpless, weak and downtrodden people. While addressing to the people at large, he would often say beggars are increasing and encouraging idealness, neither they should be given a penny nor shown mercy upon but at the same time he could not help without helping, if any beggar came him. His way of supporting the weak and the beggar was very queer. While scolding he reached them and gave him at least a sum of paper coin stealthily. Often during festival holidays like: Eid or Holi the scene of money extorting was worth seeing. His several hundred staff members surrounded him like a vast family and Nilay sir began to distribute salary bonus and advanced amount till such an extent that inspite of being so much wealth and property, there was always a big shortage of ready cash money for bringing the monetary joy to his family.

I object several times "O sir! don't be so liberal and hands free that you may drop yourself into misery". He would respond with a fresh smile. "Tulsi!" "my own family is not different to my college, you will not understand this sense of pleasure which I feel if they celebrate joyfully. I am overwhelmed with pleasure to see their happiness. I was stunned to listen his expression.

The empire of which, he was a sovereign authority had not been given by any trust committee or government. He had never received even a single penny from anybody else as donation or charity. I remember several occasions, with derision when many ministers, officers, capitalists, industrialists came as chief guest in the college function, but none had even given any smallest monetary assistance for him. Whatever he had, had been earned by his own hardest body breaking, soul rendering labour prolonged dedication to the duty and work with infinite enthusiasm, indomitable will power never ending efforts and putting his life several time at risk. Inspite of being many hundred staffs and workers, who were materialising his dreams. It was an urgent and compulsory need of administration to put watchful eye upon every issue of the college by Nilay sir in person. I have never seen any person so busy, so mentally taxed, hasty and hard working as well as happy as Nilay sir was. He had to make and put a complete command over his institutions because the time favours only those who favours his work and industry. I would often think the supreme creator had sent a very special creature on earth using enough oddities out of his universal storehouse. Nilay sir did not leave any page of his life industry unturned. He made a complete calculation of his institutional earning so that financial needs might be met out properly and timely. Everyday, several disputes from staff would be raised automatically, to which he had to convenince and dispose off. In this glorious world of supreme creator, there is a multitude of diversity among men. Shakespeare has truly termed this world as an "Unweeded Garden" perhaps, the mightiest scholar of mightiest literature was well convinced with the differences of humanity as in a natural garden, one can find all species of trees, plants, herbs and flowers including lucious jucious fruits, fragrant flowers, scented sandal wood, simultaneously briary and thorny bushes also. In the same way, an institution has all types of persons. It was not very easy for Nilay sir to run his colleges smoothly without any discussion, or dispute. At least three or four wrathful men in the guise of guardian came everyday with their complicated problems to which he had to answer.

3

Paradox and Irony of Nilay Sir

I weep several times to think about the paradox of his own life. A person who daily fought with the fatal family disputes sometimes bloody fightings, would behave with those nasty guardians with such peaceful mein and soul affecting patience that I was overwhelmed with passion to see his convincing and compromising system. Perhaps Nilay sir was well accustomed to face challenges as sorrows, and suffering have become his friends and misery his fellow companian which would sleep under one of his bed pillow. His two colleges were nearer to his residence, but one was situated eighty km away from his home in another neighbouring district namely Champawati. He had to sojourn daily, sometime by bike and often by his own self driven motor car.

It was also equally important to maintain his mental and physical health because some rude persons were afraid of nothing but to see his strong muscular heavy body, which was given by divine powers very nicely. It is universal truth that hardworking person feels hunger and strong sleep. The strong appetite is the severest feeling of human body, nothing but only food substances can satisfy a hungry man's yearning for desires.

It was the surrendered helplessness of Nilay sir to take his imbalanced and hatred fully served food to retain the power and energy of his body to make his institutions run properly so inspite of being very sensitive for his self-respect, honour and prestige, he would listen to the flood of abuses and curses let loose daily by his seven holy fire rounded wife perambulat whom her parents very rightly named Analawati Devi. She was religious, pious, merciful, tolerant, sensible, emotional and beautiful, but no sooner did she confront with Dr. Nilay her angelic affinities convert, into devilish thoughts. The roar and clamour created by her was so noiseful, vulgar and hatred ful that even a foolishman of passing routes was forced to stay listen to her debaucherous balme, which were charged everyday almost at every hour whenever Nilay sir came before her.

She was so insulting mouth bursting wench that she crossed the limits of even general respect and dignity of a common man, while entangling with Nilay sir. One thing was sure that she neither realised the goodness, greatness, sublimity and unique learning of Nilay sir nor she understood him deserved to be a great man, when the supreme powers of universal storehouse composed the being of Anala. Perhaps, they forgot to render her such great and genuine feelings to understand the learning, greatness and uniqueness of men as Dr. Nilay sir was. The cult of aesthetic beauty was totally missed from her brain. She didn't have any concern with the irony of life and its philosophy as well. Aesthetic arts to her were as to pipe before buffaloes perhaps it was the most unfortunate gift, which was accompanied with Nilay sir as a wife. She was so uncouth and rough presence that none could orally dare to teach her. She did not like to listen about any criticism concerned, behavioural speaking, or the way of living.

4

Dr. Nilay: A Profound Scholar

I was a student of nineth class. when I came in contact with Nilay sir and his family. There was a lot of discussion and rumours among the people of the city Brahmpuri. nearly twenty years ago about the educational institution of Nilay Sir. His institution imparted the education of English literature, grammar, linguistics and prosody. He inculcated the true nature of literature among students he rendered the education of English language in such a queer manner that novice could understand the hardest modes of English Grammar, if he might sit in his coaching class. He had a very unique style of teaching. There was very unique popularity of Dr. Nilay sir among his pupils someone said "Nothing is impossible for Nilay sir in English" a few said "He is the Maha Guru at English". Thus, he was taken indisputedly as "The Shakespeare of Brahmpuri; till what extent the matters of my own self is concerned I take myself a very foolish fellow. I do not have any guess of any most learned person or the depth, profoundity and the measure of Shakespeare's mind. So, I do not believe in these hyperboles. But one thing I do know that he had a unique method of expression even on the hardest topics of difficult English literature would appear very easy, when they were taught by Nilay sir.

The obscurity of W.B. Yeats, the metaphysical and personal symbols of Eliot could not bewail us due to his method of penetration, Longinus's sublime, Milton's sublimity, Bacon's aphoristic and rhetorical prose expressions, and Shakespeare's soliloquies became everlasting companion, because of his mode of unfolding the beauty of their kernals inspite of passing several storms of life over my brain-those sir's taught lessons are still retaining in my dull psyche even today.

I could not forget the day when he taught me the world famed soliloquy "what a piece of work is the man". Though, he interpreted in favour of the prince of Denmark and all human beings, but whenever his face and name are mentioned before me I could not help without asserting no doubt that he is one of the supreme creations among men of world.

5

Dr. Nilay's Optimism

I have a lot of vener and devotion for him, which kept me bound in his company since last twenty years. Though, I was a woman and my feet were shackled with the iron rods of femininty. Depite many breaks, I have continued working in his institution as a responsibleperson in-charge and teacher. There was a very deep bond of pure intimacy and belief between him and I. He relied on me too much. I have studied many philosophical uttarences proving that if a person is tempered in an atmosphere of euphoria, and comicality he turns jovial quiet contrary if any person continues suffering for a long time and gets hurt, after hurt shock, after shock, passing misery to misery and pain, to pain he becomes pessimist. But, these literary senses seem a paradox to Nilay sir, because of hundred sufferings and daily disasters, he was a stark optimist. No cloud of pessimism could shroud his brilliant rays of hope. He would always cite from The Mahabharata. "You know Tulsi, Dharmaraj Yudhisthira had once told Yaksha that a hopeless person is the driest thing of the world who can no way be enlivened in by any *sanjivine*. So, stand firmly on the massive and the most sturdy rock of hope. You will never fall dawn, when a person is aspirant and hopeful his aspiration transforms into confidence when confidence is practiced profounder it becomes self-reliance. A self reliant is the person who is directly associated with the omnipotent powers of God to remain firmly on the pivot of hope. Self confidence is likely to gain the direct support of God. Optimism gives auspicious feelings and always good consequences and he gains as he wishes, perhaps Tulsidas, the greatest poet has truly said in the *Ramayana* "*Jaki Rahi Bhawana Jaisi Prabhu Murati Dekhi Tin Taisi*". An optimistic person always finds a refuse out of universal havoc. It gives true pleasure to life and mind, because "An aspiration is a joy forever".

6

Analawati's Nature

I have spent quarter of my life in his institution and due to my complete devotion. I have always tried to understand the new comers and others who have joined the college. I know nearly two hundred academic and non–academic staff members. I understood nearly all of them more or less. But, I could not understand Analawati, the earliest married wife of Nilay sir. Her nature and behaviour was like a revolving disc, one can confront her with several facets of single nature within a week. Like C.I.D. I have kept my watchful eyes upon the issues of her college and home but failed to understand her quarrelsome and wrathful nature. She always appeared very cool and calm. Whenever I met her and my meeting was in calm atmosphere. None could claim her to be harmful or ill-tempered to anyone in any way rather, she was very gentle, religious, social, unfashionable, egoless and liberal. She did not drop even the drop of water in her throat without worshiping God. She had no vanity, no prejudice, no pride or malice for anybody else. She was very charitable and generous. Although, she was a wife of a very rich learned and famous person but she did not have any notion of richness or greatness. She would go for shopping accompanied with labourers and very poor men's wives. She had a intimacy with poor hawkers and rickshaw puller and she joined their company very joyfully, but these virtues seem oxymoron when she came vis-a-vis with Dr. Nilay.

7

The Horrible Conflict

Everyday in the early morning Nilay Sir would leave home for his institutions. Anala throughout the day lived at the home, happily ate, drank whatever she liked made a lot of gossip with neighbouring rustic wenches, but as soon as Nilay Sir came to the home she burned with fury on very trivial issues and made heart-rendering shriek daily at any or other time holding the common duties of her home. She always started the dispute from a very little cause, but it took a very fierce form in spite of being very wise and learned Nilay sir broke the boundaries of self-respect and honour, while entangling with her. The war of words was very obscene between them Verbal conflict always ended with physical assault. I have noticed that Nilay sir had pungently worthful nature or perhaps, he had been transformed by the venomous conduct of Anala. The regular hurt of physical and mental strike had made Nilay sir a parched and burnt tree of forest fire. I remained much worried thinking about their future. Often I have spent my nights sleepless thinking about the bridal life of modern men. The experience of Nilay Sir's life had filled in my mind a lot of dejection, indifference and hatred for marriage I would pray to God "O divine powers! If these are the joys of a married life, make me always a bachelor. I forgot to think about married life, but I did not feel any little pleasure out of conflict. I had a lot of sympathy for them. I have pledged for myself "I will find out the cause of turmoil." So, I began to look into the lives of both persons and did my utmost attempt to judge the bone of contention.

8

Tulsi: The Narrator

As I was dwelling in another apartment of his own house building. Nilay sir and his family dwelt in the ground floor, so all voices, quarrels, uproar and clamour reach my ears clearly daily for sometime, Anala avoided my presence, but after Sona's episode she became a complete shameless and free-spoken rustic woman, who was always ready to pour the flood of curses and abuses at the 'Ulysses' of Brahmpuri. I felt a lot of pain, I was extremely sorry perceiving such behaviour with the man, who was good for everything. But, I couldn't do anything, I was living at her mercy in his own home. I was too much obliged to her to allow me to live in her own building, to a woman who was in no way better than an orphan and helpless creature. I have a very rough exterior and I am not a beauty in any way; my tanned, wrinkled face and dark complexion was in no way envious for her instinct. So, she never objected at my survival. Anala was so dominating and aggressive speaker that no member of whole staff could dare to interrupt her voice.

I was suffering badly from dilemma. It was very pinching and troubling that I was unable to find out the reasons of discord after many efforts I found few of the root causes of disharmony between Dr. Nilay and Analawati Devi, which I assessed are thus noteworthy to mention widely for readers to understand well about the nature of their dispute.

9

The Cause of Disharmony

The first and foremost alarming reason that I gazed was a big gulf between their mental standards 'In the name of God'. I enumerate that Nilay sir was so far superior in the field of knowledge, worldly wisdom and practical commonsense that Anala appeared just like a foolish girl of a primary school and he was a skilled University topper. In the matters of intellect, brilliance, talent and thought it is merely wastage of mental energy to analyse Anala with Dr. Nilay. Their humours were wide apart, nothing but intellect appealing topics could provoke laughter for him while she often laughed over rough, vulgar and foolish issues. In the matter of academic education, she was ten and he was ton. Broadly speaking. Anala was merely literate and was not able to read her mothertongue Hindi properly, while Nilay sir was gifted uniquely by Muse with double MAs, B. Ed and Doctorate in English literature, i.e., Ph.D. After many efforts once in a complete privacy, Nilay sir had described how he was got caught with this woman. During marriage Nilay sir was only an innocent boy and very sober student of tenth class. He did not know more about the world, its enticements, prudery and hypocrisy. He told me that he only questioned once about Anala's education, it was told by her step-mother to sir that she was also studying in ninth class. After marriage, Nilay sir came to know that she was only literate and left her studies when she was in class second. Out of several prolonged verbal discourses, I came to know that perhaps during Nilay sir's pre-marriage period the family status of him was not very prestigious. It seems to me as if the arranged, marriages were not very easy to happen in Nilay sir's family. Very few persons visited his home to marry their daughters with his young generation. It was considered perhaps, by sir's family members that it is the luckiest chance for a young man to demand someone marry and accept him as son-in-law. So, when Anala's father Jagdish Prasad (Jagga) put the proposal before Nilay sir, he was overwhelmed with joy. Though he didn't know what marriage meant in actual senses and said to his extremely crooked and cunning father-in law, "I will marry with your daughter, Nothing could stop me".

I often burst into laughter when, I remember his confession how he prayed and fasted several times in many temples to find Anala as his wife. In this way he committed himself totally responsible to accept this boorish companion.

Nilay sir was a profound reader and deep student of several literatures he never stopped studying as he said often among pupils, students and staff members, "Don't think to stop studies at any end of life because the field of knowledge is like vast ocean which will never cease to pour its water of knowledge and wisdom. Education is the ever running process which will continue to run-up to the end of life of any man's ultimate eternity".

There was not more difference between his saying and doing so he studied a lot and became a master of several streams of knowledge. Due to intellectual gap, Dr. Nilay and Anala were never agreed at any matter and quarrelled always on account of this disharmony. I am the eye witness of such broils God knows why Anala never liked to put her surrender before any controversy. The reason of disapproval was perhaps a mania of Analawati Devi she strictly practised and was well aware about the sense of superiority. She never accepted any household goods without putting several unapproved crucial questions.

The second reason what I metered was the heavy epidemic hovering doubts, which damaged the yearning desires of love and lust between she and him. Doubt is the most injuring insect in relation of any person's life, where is the matter of matrimonial bond-it is the most heinous feeling which hallows out the flowering relation of any husband and wife within few days. It is the invincible rust, which can never be washed by any strongest acid. The sting of doubt is so malicious that no *sanjeevani* can heal it up. Quite contrary, faith is the vital source of nuptial relations. It is the integral part of love, honour and dedication. Faith is invicible, which always gains, victory out of all types of conflicts.

10

Dr. Nilay's Prosperity

Nilay sir was hardly passing thirty five years of his life, while he had accumulated the material prosperity of more than hundred crore. His fastest growth was due to the loan amounts taken from several banks. He had a very strong credit of a payee who never missed even a single premium to pay timely. So all the banks honoured him and preferred to accept Nilay sir as his customer. He was much more laden under a heavy load of unpaid bank debts. These loan amounts were the chief cause of tension and worry for Nilay sir, though he was well confidant about their fulfilment. Once a bank manager cynically asked him "what will you do if your educational institutions go flop." He replied in a very grim voice, "I can pay your debt sir by running small coaching classes and by providing individual tuitions to the students if my institutions fail". Looking his howling sense of self- confidence, the manager got fused with nice feelings and always treated very nicely with Nilay sir whenever he visited his office in the bank. Inspite of this confidence, his worry about the loan amounts was never less. The heart rendering mental anguish and his uncompromising life partner's hidden and silent tortures troubled him so much at time to time that he frequently willed to run away somewhere unknown to anyone, but he couldn't do so. He was rather helpless to do so. It was his grim helplessness, which kept him always bounded with his family and birthplace. He knew well that if he ran away by leaving his workhouse in such state of debt, the consequences would be fatal; because if the premiums and the installment were not filled and paid timely, most of his property would be usurped by banks. Thus, he was badly forced to maintain his material property he could not run else away any where. In this way he listened to the harsh, hoarse and vulgarly diffused words of his ritually bonded wife mutely.

11

Dr. Nilay's Helplessness

Several problems and challenges arose in Nilay sir's activities, but psychologically he could practise paradox in outer and inner state of his mind. Not only it was necessary to appear normal rather it was equally very necessary to retain the balance and patience of his mind, because his one impatient act could give him a very serious hurt. So despite holding a burning cinder into his heart outwordly he looked as cool and calm as any *yogi,* actually sir was helpless.

Sleep has been called the balm of afflicted soul by Shakespeare and nature's second great soothing gift the joyest meal of life feast. A good sleep is the direct source of a good health and good mental poise and balance, though sleep is equally important for human beings. But, it is extremely and vitally necessary for mental and thoughtful diligents. Often our well wishers wish; "sweet sleep and good dreams". But Nilay sir hardly slept ever peacefully during twenty-four years of his diligent life of post-marital period. Often, very crucial and bitter quarrels took place over night during bed time. And thus he would often spend his whole nights sleepless. For God's sake, I tell you O' gentle and divinely sentimental readers that Anala never left any terrible cause to discuss obscenely during bed time; claiming scandalous affairs of several women with him. She suspects so deeply at him that even motherly and sisterly meetings of Nilay sir with any woman appeared to her as an incestuous relation. The words spoken by her were so hard; pinching and brain scorching, harshing and harrassing that Nilay sir has also violated his mental control and began to cry, applying his loathsome anger vice-versa. The acute verbal seminar of scandalism found no stop throughout night till the crimson sunlight in the eastern corridor had dawned.

Nilay sir was helpless to lie on bed and further he had to rise up to go for handling his workhouse. Having seen his face and unsleepy physical appearance, if some of his well wishing staff members asked about his disturbed look and behaviour, he cleverly pretended before his attendants and workers claiming about this or that mishap which had awakened him in the night and took unwilling naps to rid off his drowsy and red-eye orbs.

Often Nilay sir appeared terribly thoughtful and tensioned thinking about his material prosperity. I commemorate over his assertions when he said, "Tulsi, I want to stop all my institutions altogether. What is the use and good of this labour and sufferings. If there is no peace or happiness to me". But in the mean time, he grew very sentimental-thinking about the fond employees and their jubilant life,whose chief source was his institution-sir was extremely forced to continue his educational industry,which was equally a celetial source of service for mankind because it was the super-speciality of his academic and professional institution, not only to render into the minds of students, bookish knowledge and purpose ful-skill, but also to impart them, the human values, moral values, the need of a good character, nice conduct and loving behaviour. He would often say among his students during morning assembly "Dear students! gaining bookish knowledge is necessary, having professional skill is compulsory but being morally rich is vital. A person devoid of human values, moral values, good conduct, nice character and unshakable faith in God is no better than a trained animal.So we must be materially progressive and spiritually rich, only then we can descend the Heaven on Earth and make our life happy in the true senses.

Because, his institutions were the source of earning and livelihood of several people. So he, did not want to snatch the bread and the pleasure of people's life by stopping his industry on the middle of its apex. Obviously, Nilay sir was helpless to live for others. Despite several teachers and highly qualified teaching body, Nilay sir himself taught daily for twenty or thirty minutes in all of his three educational branches. He was a born teacher and teaching was a passion for him. He couldn't be happy without teaching daily inspite of being a unique teacher, he was a profound scholar of English language and literature as well. He was a great moral preacher and possessed an enormus knowledge about God, nature, religion, humanity, womanhood and childhood and practical wisdom, the Ramayana, the Geeta, the Mahabharata, the Bible, Greek stories and several ethical, mythical and legendary books of Hinduism, Sanskrit and Hindi literature. He was a best orator, anchor, actor, humourist, humanist and a poet at heart. His schools and colleges were the best platform to perform talents and whenever found time, he would unfold his knowledge and brilliance before his teachers and students, which would satisfy him very much. So, he tolerated Christly the mischief, insults and bitter welcome of his seven lives, booned wife regularly without disturbing any sect of his work. Thus, inspite of thinking several times to run away stealthily to unknown place without prior information to anyone couldn't work out. He was seized and enveloped in his fond institutions so lovingly that he could not flee anywhere. He had a very heavy compulsion to stay there among his retinue.

How could Nilay sir let his blood stained labour's fruit ruining? !!!

PART–II

12

Early Marriage

As I had told you while describing cursorily about Dr. Nilay sir. I again tell you that Nilay sir was merely a school-going boy of tenth class approximately fourteen years of age, when he childishly accepted the marriage proposal of cunning parents who secretly, wedded his only uncouth daughter Anala very hastily- hotly with him who had a certificate of eighth passed though she couldn't read and write even Hindi letters well .. It was told to Nilay sir that she was also studying in ninth class so sir was convinced thinking that she can be taught forward and he agreed to the proposal and the predestined adversary of Dr. Nilay became his wife.

It was the province of north zone of the holy great and incredible India namely, Uttar Pradesh, the birth place of Lord Rama and Krishna whose only district Brahmpuri was found fit by the God of decree to give birth to Nilay. The tragic story of Nilay sir was much more caused due to his simple innocent and wordly-failed parents as well as family members. Marriage of a son was considered as the biggest achievement of life, whether the match might be proper or improper. Sir's father Pandit Radhey Shyam was very simple-natured, innocent and good for everything as well as a thorough-going gentleman.

12

13

The Improper Bounties

Oh! God you have made a very nice world, enriched with multitude of nice things, enveloped this world with lush green beautiful celestial and attractive nature. It sounds with bubbling and gurgling of sonorous rivers and waterfalls. You have made it pregnant with luscious and jucy fruits, wombed with jewels and golds, scattering fragrant flowers, plants, herbs, birds and unnumbered species of trees. It is equally lovable and charming to the "Eden Garden of the Paradise, particularly created by God for his first and prime issues, Adam and Eve. Oh! Saviour of humble folk, your world has so many colours, figures and features. It seems the most appropriate place for humanity to dwell perhaps heaven will also not be so pleasant, so soothing, so advantageous and usĕful, so lovely as your planet Earth is purposely gifted to mankind to work, to live and to play. But, there is a blunder on your part concerned to earth as you have filled this world with rogues, frauds, corrupt, cunning and loath some morons and ruffans. Here, the good men are rarely rare. Oh! Almighty God! Will your world ever be ready to receive thy saints and gentles? How long! Oh Lord! How Long! Oh lord! How far! Oh God! How far! Your world has well been described in these Hindi verses:

"Veshyana ko roop dinhon!!
Ratnakar khar kinhon!!
Nain diyo mriga ko!!
Sugandh sona na diyo!!
Kabul so desh jahan!!
Mughal pachharain dhenu!!
Wahan diyo mewa!!
Kareel Brij mein diyo!!
Bade-bade guniyan ko!!
Phirawat ho dwar-dwar!!
Gun te vihin tinhen!!
Nek sampada diyo!!
Kaun-kaun chook main!!
Bakhano ek anan te!!
Nam chaturanan par!!
Chookto chaley gayo!!"

Undoubtedly, this world is not fit and favourable to live for men like Radhey Shyam, who can easily be deceived by enticements of such persons like Jagga, the father-in-law of Nilay sir.

Jagdish Prasad, whom people notoriously called "Jagga" was a multi-branched criminal of his district Bailwaria, who had committed all sorts of crimes, since his very adolescence. Blood shed and fighting was a routine, who spoke nothing but abuse. He had a very quarrelsome and firy nature. He was foolish chatter and an audacious perverter of truth. He was so angry aggressive and dominant by nature in behaviour and personality that was enough to make several joyful faces weep during any social ceremony as marriage or religious rituals. Jagga had to leave his home district Bailwariya, because of his ill activities and took job in the paper mill of district Brahmapuri which was nearly four hundred km away from home. We can say it, as the dominant role of fate and chance which encountered Jagga with Radhey Shyam and Anala with Nilay simultaneously. No doubt, some invisible forces always work behind the life of a man about whom it has been said "Purposive unmotivated dominant thing which sways in dark way faring". Or in the words of the King Lear "As flies to the wanton boys, so we to the Gods (fate and chance), they kill us for their mere sport".

Jagga had a relative nearing the neighbouring block of Radhey Shyam's colony. Thus, one day during a religious ceremony namely Lord *Satya Narayan Ji ki katha,* the crooked family met with an innocently foolish Pandit Radhey Shyam's third son, who was specifically and exquisitely incarnated as the boon of God namely Nilay was faced by these hyppocritical persons of eastern Uttar Pradesh region. According to Nilay sir's mothers a good wife is so important for a man's life that one should face a deadly battle to gain her. Whenever I found chance, I asked this question to sir "Is your wife the cause of your suffering? Are wives pain-creating and subject to botheration of any husband's life? Then, men must not marry, 'sir'. They must remain bechelor and a known individual. Good, great and gentle man should never have a wife."

14

The Uniqueness of Wife

Having heard this blameful utterance, Nilay sir became philosophically grave. He heavily objected at my expression and began to depict the goodness and uniqueness of a wife in any husband's life.

Dr. Nilay said "Tulsi, don't speak like this wives are not the chief source of misery for husbands rather they are psychological-physician an e-healer who remove tensions of men's mind. It has been well said that a good life and a good wife is gained by none but only the most fortunate ones because-some women are so devilish that they transform even the divine-natured man into a fine ruffian. The life turns into a hell and home becomes a graveyard.

With the deepest sigh, Nilay sir said "Oh! Tulsi, you are quiet ignorant about the superb role and divine contribution of sensible life follower. A good wife is the most valuable, the nicest and the best gift of God given to any man on Earth. Generally, people say that a woman cannot lead a good life without a husband-man but the assertion is quite, wrong. It sounds some paradoxical statement. In true sense, the survival of a good life is impossible for the husband-man without a good wife. A good wife is the truest and the most devoted well-wisher, nurse, unique friend, genuine teacher, superb guardian, supreme counsellor and a complete ignition system in a man's life machinery. Her true love, unchangeable care and sentimentally passionate affection removes all sorts of hurdles and hindrances of life. Even the longest life seems very short in a gentle wife's sweet company. Howsoever tough, hard and complicated problem it may be, but a good wife's loving co-operation and powerful assurance removes it away very easily. She is just like an elixir of celestial love, who awakes the dying powers of a man. She is all beauty and total loveliness of a husband's home. She always sustains the life of her husband with acute approval. She generates new creative ideas and operates them in her most sensible manners. A true wife is an everlasting companion and a ceaseless source of support and cooperation in the life journey of a husbandman. A gentle wife has most authentically been called the *Griha Laxmi,* i.e., the Goddess of wealth in home because she paves the path which brings wealth and possesions into the home of a man. A real wife is shrewd and true judge of her husband's nature, who can well and most excellently understand the mood and temperament of her husband in the state of any misery, trouble or melonchaly. Although, a devoted wife has been called one of the wheels of domestic carriage, but she is the wheel which can goad the carriage of life to run towards the proper direction of all sorts of progress and upliftment.

It is very ridiculous to call a woman '*Abala*' i.e., weak in powers, but in true senses a good chaste and able wife is the perennial source of all kinds of powers i.e., mental, physical and spiritual. A genuine life partner enhances the mental and intellectual powers of her husband by sharing good ideas treasured in her noble heart in the state of tranquil privacy. She makes husband physically fit, active and healthy by providing and persuing to eat balanced food diet. She performs all kinds of religious ceremonies, moral and divine ritualistic duties better than men thus she enlarges the spiritual powers of her family and makes her husband convinced that God is always with us. We are no way alone in this huge tempestuous havocful life journey on this happy Earth.

A good wife is not only the rarest dowry, but also she is that rising stairesteps of any man's material, physical, intellectual and mental developments with whose loving and kind support. He can easily gain versatile properities in a sportive manner. It has been well said in this famous Hindi poem 'Jeevan Sangini'—

"Maya dhan pad swasthya aru
Jeeta sakal jahan
Binu pyari sangini ke
Sab dhan dhuri saman
Sab dhan dhuri saman
Jagat mein kachhu na bhavai
Din bhar rahai udas
Rudan kari rain bitavai
Madhuras vyanjan dhare
Lagai sabheen kuch feenka
Bina sulaxan nari
Jagat ye lagai na neeka
Gavain geet "Abodha"
Suno ho Thakur man ke
Binu sundari piriti
Ginai na koi ganke."

15

An Humble Begging

O! Merciful God Almighty! the Saviour of humble folk! Omni-present! Omniscient! and the Omnipotent! Oh! Creator of vast world and multitude of creatures! O! Farmer of unique nature! O! Supreme producer of life! O! maker of all! and marrer of every thing. It is the most humble prayer of mine O! The most gracious friend of mankind! Give every thing fair or foul of man according to their object and disposition of duties as well as the result of their pre and natal existences. But never unite a good worthy gentle and learned man with an uneducated and boorish woman what so ever, for the sin he had committed in his previous life, punish him in any other way. But don't bless him with an uncouth life companion, because it will be fatal, curse and profound, suffering which will break his nerve and make him an everlastingly sick forever and unfated person.

The stinging behaviour of an evil-wife for a good man is more poisonous and pain creating than any other venom on earth. If a good wife is the most gracious Goddess, yet contrarily an evil wife is more fierce witch than the obnoxious witches which nothing but only the vast hell can hold. Howsoever strong bodied wrestler type of good man he may be, he proves like a lout, helpless and feeble before a wicked and villainous wife, who can do nothing but to bear the tortures, torments and treachery of his wife like a dumb spectator. Thus, it is awefully difficult for a gentle learned and socially prestigious husband to live with an evil woman together. I was moved with enormous passions and pity listening to his superb glorification of wife and womanhood. Dr. Nilay sir was at that time looking very emotional and despondent. The overwhelming passion was heavily and heavily occupied on his mind. He was under the deep philosophical deliverance.

16

Moral Helplessness

Sir continued, "Tulsi! I take it as good sense in some matters, the divorce system of western Christians and Muslims, but the country like ours and for the men like Dr. Nilay gentle respectable Hindu Brahmin, the marriage is the holiest bond only once entangling thread which gets catch so fervently pressed thing that parting is impossible. Break in Hindu marriage and divorces are the most controversial issue in our country. When once enveloped to gentle, learned and prestegious persons particularly Hindus, it leaves only after being merged with eternity. Divorces cannot be so easily practised. A wife in our country is considered the seven lives retained companion whose bond is purified by taking seven sleepy round of the holy fire during the performance of rituals belonging to Vedic concept by drowsy priests and Pandits in the midnight. In a gentle society. taking divorce is the farthest. It is considered a great sin to think about even in dreams. So whatsoever type, woman one's wife may be but once being wedded, it is nearly impossible to secure separate maintenance for reputed gentle persons particularly in a reputed Hindu family, especially with the men of upper castes. Our wise and prudent society doesn't allow also a boy and girl before their marriage. Often marriages are based on only assumptions and speculative expectations whether any of the two persons proves far superior in knowledge, intellect, talent, wisdom and mental standards after marriage, he/she can't proclaim about these antipathies after marriage. So howsoever uncouth, ill and boor type of a woman/man, may be worthy and gentle woman/ man is forced socially, morally and religiously to live and survive with her/him.

17
Brutality for Women

"Tulsi" my dear daughter' "you have not understood this modern time through its actual spectacles. I accept oathfully that women are neither safe, nor secure, nor happy. Family violences have become a very common thing. No doubt, they are oppressed, troubled and tortured everywhere. Out of hundred matrimonial disputes ninety nine percent women appear to be suffering and exploited victims. How I curse and what can I say about those greedy money loving devilish husband-men and their family animals who burn the young brides in their homes on being failed to fulfill their monetary demands. How should I tell you how often I get heavily disturbed reading the news of innocent ladies' tragic lot. But the omni-doer God is the biggest judge one can escape from earthly courts and manual writs and appeals, but he shall in no way be escaped from the supreme judiciary of heaven. The consequences of such brutal acts will be fatally sorrowful. My heart suffers with infinite anguish and profound torments, when I hear any such brutal act of killing a feeble gentle, coyful and educated lady for dowry. The law boards all over the world must agree on this ground for giving heaviest pannel punishments for such sinful crime perpetrators. During my long teaching career, I have met with several gentle women folk who were so tenderly frail in physical forms though grandouerly rich in inward qualities that even a harsh and dashing voice can make them swoon. There were some such person who did not know, express any simple ill word. There are the few to whom a scolding can make speechless. I have confronted with several ladies so meek, pious, charitable, coy, innocent feeble and physically extremely beautiful that it is quiet impossible to think of any forceful dispute will be caused by them. I was suffocated with impulses and sentiments listening to views of several divinely-framed women that they can prefer to die than being entangled with any controversy. The world would be a hallow brag, if the Almighty had not created these creatures of beauty, loveliness, innocence and an apostle of patience, sacrifice, labour and love.

18

Greatness of Woman

Having expressed such opinions sir became much thoughtful and completely silent, while I began to think about his genuine faith in the power and contribution of women. My life has passed through several miseries and pains. My parents and brothers have done a lot of injustice with me being an unmarried woman I was also troubled and tortured very much. My parents did not want to educate me but I wanted to gain higher education. My family members beat me, starved me and gave no financial aid to me. Once I opened my heart to sir about my miseries when he convinced me by gifting this poem about woman's supremacy.

"Hey! Mamta, Ramani, Premmayi
Hey! Putri Bhagini, Hey! Bharya
Hey! Divya Shakti, Hey! Mahashakti
Vatsalya, Mamatva Amit Arya!!

Tuhi Durga, Tuhi Laxmi
Tuhi hai Rahchandi Kali
Tu Paramshakti tu Yog Shakti
Tuhi Jan Pushpo ki Mali

Tu Udbhava, Sthiti Pralaya Roop
Palak Poshak Sanharak hai
Eksha se Teri Vidhi Hari Har
Sansar Karya Parichalak Hai!!
Tu Seeta si Vanvashini Hai
Meera Ban Vish ki pyasini hai
Draupadi Sadrish Tu Sahti hai
Is Jag Mein Apna Cheer haran
Tu Kabhi Sukho ki na bhukhi
Karti hai Dukho Kalesh Varan

Tu Dharti hai dharitri hai
Ratano ki Khan Maharati hai
Tu Satyavan Savitri hai
Maha devi sam kaviyatri hai

Tu abala nahi purna bal hai
Tu simit nahi amit jal hai.
Unnant annant roop tera
Kada tera sabse uncha hai
Tu mahajano mein mahantam
Teri astitva samoochan hai
Brahmand niketa prabhuvar ne
Jab ye brahmand banaya tha
Adbhuta sanyam Dheeraj Lekar
Naritva Roop ko Paya Tha

Yadi Panch Pati ke Hote Bhi
Draupadi Neerih Ho Gayi Thi
Yadi Garbha Kal Mein Seeta si
Satvanti Ban-Ban Royi Thi
Yadi Emile Dickinson Jeevan Bhar
Mar Mar Kar Maut Bulaati Rahi
Laxmi Bai Si Ranchandi
Jeevan Bhar Choten khati rahi
Yati Sati Chenamma Kood Padi
Thi Dhak-Dhak Karti Jwala Mein
Yadi Gargi Ne Udghosh Sahe
Ashru Si Bahi Apala Ne
To Hey! Devi Tu Kyun Vyakul
Dukh Tera Nahi Akela Hai
Jeevan Mein Mrityu
Sukhon Mein Dukh
Yaha Dhoop Chanva Ka Mela Hai
Jo Ghatata Hai Wo Badhta Hai
Jo Girta Hai Wo Uthata Hai.
Jo Rota hai Wo Hasta Hai
Jo Ujada Gaya wo Basta Hai
Sahi Kar Jeevan Ki Dhoop Chhanva
Jo Mann Vichalit Nahi Karta Hai
Usne samjha Jeeva Dharshan
Woh ManmaujiAlmasta Hai

Ugata Huva suraj Lal Dikhe
Doobe bhi arun dikhlata hai
Waha Hi Hai Sachcha Manuja Yaha
Jo Ek sadrish Raha Jata Hai.

Isliye Tyag Kar Mano Vyatha
Santosh Hridaya Mein Dhariyega
Raghuveer Harenge Sab sankat.
Devi Tu Dheeraj Dhariyega".

I have hardly completed the reading of the poem, in the mean time sir again came to me and started his narration about woman being.

19

Wicked Woman

"Despite the unique goodness of women beings; there are some exceptions, though I say firmly that those exceptional fishes, cannot make the whole pond dirty. Exceptions will remain as exceptions, but the wife or woman like Analawati Devi, the blessed and booned wife of mine is rarely rare.

Perhaps, none ever properly tried to look into such matters very deeply and seriously that in this male dominant society, some-where few gentlemen are the most miserable and suffering victims. Their lives are so badly shackled and chained with moral, filial, professional and social duties that they bear with endless pain and heart rendering sorrow and can do nothing to stop their wives' brutality.

"O! Tulsi today I am not in normal senses. I tell you how Anala threatens and blackmails me. "Nearly after every painful discussion, nothing knocks me so badly down as her frightening words of false threats about disclosing the scandalous affairs, which were never been concerned. Once she said, "I am going in public places of your reputed city to tell among the people of common and uncommon status as well as the court personnel about your mischief to have kept me as a servant taking, all working giving nothing but beating me like a best, if I don't work. I will tell the whole world about your loose characterness. It will destroy your whole status and will perish your all honour in the dust by saying that you are dissolute. I will cry with my full throat pitched coming in your prestigious office of the main branch that you demand money by advising to go to spend nights with other men, you have forced me for prostitution, thus I will damage your whole reputation among the people where you are worshipped like deity. Everybody will spit at your mouth then just imagine about that horrible scene. O! pig you shall die with shame and endless remorse".

I rolled down from my chair listening to this obnoxious narration and was so perturbed about sir's anguish that my eyes began to shed tears automatically. I said I cannot........ "Sir" "I am not an angel like you" but Nilay sir was so despondent and moody and that he interrupted and began to tell me about another terrible event, when Anala demoralised very heniously and degraded him. After mutual despute, she gathered many unfavourable persons of neighbourhood. Nilay sir was standing on the open balcony of his ground floor and she was below the roof raising a finger at him. She said, "O! Brothers and sisters of my neighbourhood! Do you know this heavy bodied male-buffalo?. He is my husband unfortunate! Listen carefully you consider him as a gentle learned teacher. Today, I will tell you the truth what he is, in actual senses as I have seen him throughout twenty five years. Never believe on this man as a chaste and characterised one. This dirty dog of a backward village is always busy in his school office in gazing sexy *laundiyas* (young girls) their body, face, cheeks and chins. O God! Condemn on this ghastily mean. Even the tabla playing louts, who make their sisters, daughters and wives dance before the drunken spectators and do the business of their bodies, are not so shameless as this debauchee. Never call him sir. He cannot be called an animal, as they are not as demoralisingly dirty as this one is. He must be buried alive upto shoulders leaving the head open on any public chauraha (square) where some dirty shoes of any stagnant water thrown must be kept to beat his head by the passersby; the punishment will be less than what he deserves".

20

Endless Suffering

After this narration, sir was looking very grim, heavy, perturbed and swollen. In a very pitiable tragic voice, He lastly said, “She has truely shown my character, I am really a very abhorred spirit of Satan’s Hell world”. After this expression, sir could not stay with me anymore he needed tranquility as he would often sit lonely thinking very seriously about his future life and the institution. Sitting for hours alone he became somewhat lightened, but was too intemperate that he couldn’t remain silent. Once again he addressed me with a deep daughterly affection and began to narrate the humble lot of some gentle husbands in the cruel clutches of their insensible brutal wives. ‘Tulsi’ “the fact can’t be avoided. It is absolutely right that some gentle reputed as well as prosperous men tolerate infinite troubles and tortures mentally and physically both offered by their innocent woes gays companions and speak nothing like dumb puppets. Their masculine vigour, power, prestige, name and social authority forbid them expose soul-rendering and bark peeling enimities of their wives.

“They work hard mentally as well as physically throughout the day and sometimes they starve the whole day in the haste of maintaining and holding their business and profession well and when they return home in the evening in search of rest, peace, love and food. They are badly disturbed and horrified by their rude life partners, mostly they spend their nights so discomfortly and sleeplessly that they wake up in the morning as sapped out patient of chronic jaundice. Somehow if, their bloody nights are intrigued by someone and if any of their wellwishers questions about that state of mind and physique they laugh ironically and pretend that it was the rough dialogue of a telecast film not the quarrell of their owns. How can such husband-men survive and in what way they pretend".

"No hurt is more retaining and stinging than the hearts' hurt. No thrashing is worse than indecent, vulgar and ominous words spoken by their pretty darlings."

21

The Panic of Legal System

O Tulsi! "the próblem is not sustained only by rude wives, the law also plays a very damaging role."

Our legal system adds more fuel to this injustice, the very announcement of law brings any most terrified scene of nightmare for gentle husband-men. A reputed man gets stunned hearing about Indian Panel Code (IPC) passed by prudent politicians, thinking nothing about the side effects, pros and cons. As soon as any wicked wife threatens a gentle husband announcing about law, he begins to shudder like an aspen leaf."

"The law stands always in favour of women, because in most of the family, voilences i.e., the matter of husband-wives, the wives are sufferers and a tortured victim. Since the very dawn of Indian human civilization, the women have been the sole victims of their brutal husbands', treachery, anarchy and injustice. Mostly women are tortured and exploited by the members of their in-laws house or husband-man. Dowry act, women torture act, women society and National Women Commission are just like an electrical shock for gentlemen. They are enough support for a cunning and a rude wife to totally destroy these humble personages only by reminding about such security acts. Thus, few husband-men are always threatened and blackmailed with all sorts of tourture and exploitations in the name of these women defending bills. It is very easy for a wicked wife to announce the privacy of matrimonial life before uncounth persons but most of the men are very shy and feel a lot of insult to expose the walled affairs of their life before public. But inspite of narrating the woeful tale they gave no response in his favour Abdul Raheem Khane-Khana a great Indian religious poet of Hindi Literature has well said in this couplet—

"Rahiman nij mann ki byatha

Mann he rakho goya

Suni athi laihain log sab

banti na lenhai koya."

Nearly the gentle and learned readers will agree with the fact that very few persons will affirm with this paradoxical truth that a poor, tender and a lanky frame of a woman can also torture a hardy-hooded muscular body of a male person. Often people take keen interest in listening to the vulgur narration of one's married couple dispute, when it is narrated by a woman in a very supportive manner adding more fuel to the fire, but neither a man can narrate nor the other people will listen eagerly. The women have been considered as the most sacrificing and utmostly laborious being, if they make a commitment to hold the responsibilities they pay the oath unto the edge of doom. Quiet contrary, if any woman firmly decides to derail any management they show their it most carelessness. No doubt, the wicked wives are totally careless about their domestic duties. So, they have a lot of time to plan and conspirate against busy husband but at the same time, a gentleman cannot do that. Thus, the society and people all around always turn in favour of woman and industrious man is always ignored in taking the favour of his neighbours in the comparison of evil wife".

22

The Perils of Divorce

I was overburdened with pity and sympathy. Though, I never thought to destroy the relation of any couple even in dream, I never wished any-body else to have any legal separati on, but sir's matter was very eerie and one of the rarest types of husband-wife relation so one day I blurted out, O! sir ,"You must gain a legal separation from Anala madam, she must be divorced". "As soon as the very word "divorce" came out from my mouth, he began to look as thoughtful, pale and nervous as Lord Buddha having seen the scene of dead person and its cremation as described by Sir Edwin Arnold in his great epic 'Light of Asia' book-(III). With a deep sigh, Nilay sir further began to speak about his prudent ideas concerned about marriage break and divorce Thus. O! Tulsi, how can it be so? It is the heinous sin which can never be redeemed. There are many devastating perils which are unceasingly associated with divorce".

Perhaps divorce cannot be so harmful, if taken in the beginning of one or two years after marriage. But, the contradiction between the new couples are always solved forcely by family folks in the beginning and expect nicety for future but in the hope of amendment, often many years roll away, the delayed estrangement leaves a very damaging influence on both persons. It becomes heinous crime, if the couple have some children. The marriage breaks after begetting children is very fatal, it makes young children's lives chaotic often such children turn into dull- minded and sometimes go abnormal. Nothing is so precious and dear for young children as their mother and father are. A child wants the company of both simultaneously, as two eyes look one object one similarly both mother and father are equally loving dear and desirable for the kids. The separation of mom and dad is effecting very disastrously to him/her. There are some children who are so sensitive and delicate that they die prematurely after their parents got divorced. An innocent child is like Lord Hanuman for whom Rama (Father) and Sita (Mother) are equally important, lovely and joyful".

"There are so many liabilities and financial problems which make the situation very critical, if the divorces are practised very lately".

On considering this burning issue on social and moral grounds, it can be proclaimed that divorce, is in no way a good thing. It is neither in the favour of husband nor wife. It is never good or desirable for a good society, nation, culture or for humanity. So, it is stamped that it should never be practised in a civilised society."

23

Uncompromisable Terms

With a little pause, Sir further continued—

"But sometimes, "Tulsi" the marriage state becomes so critical, difficult, arduous to survive that if divorce is not practised, it can change a good man into a criminal, a murderer who does not only destroy his own talents will be but, a great peril for the society and human race.

Man is the supreme creation of God, who possess unique faculties of head and heart, the paragon of virtues, the beauty of the world, a creature of angelic actions is much more guided by his own emotions and passions. Howsoever reasonable and logical person one can be, any or other time he must be impulsive or sentimental. A man devoid of sentiments, emotions and feelings is no way a man. He must be termed a two-legged varied animal. So, when a man unites with a dry inspid-hearted unemotional woman, he cannot be contended any least in her company". "Aprosperous, industrious and a successful man is surrounded by many men and women in his business and professional life, but if a woman takes it very pungently and bitterly bad and makes a lot of hue and cry and draws a line of divison, if she conditionally urges to her husband." Either live with your fellows and staff members or with her" how can a succeeding man stay in her company". "Human life, health, body and personality are the best boons of God for one who possessed them magnificently. Most of the people are careless about their fitness, smartness, physical charms and for taking nutritious food. It is their own ways of leading lives, but some persons are very careful about making and retaining their physique, active, smart and good looking ,for this purpose and they take good food, fruits, do proper physical exercise, balance their routine and thus they try to look ever young and handsome quiet contrary if someone's wife is completely careless about her physical, mental fitness and about balanced diet and shows a lot of jealousy with her husband's *'Chir Tarunya ki sadhna'* (the hard attempt of making himself ever young and maintained). If the uncouth, unroutined and self centred careless wife of an exercising healthy, smart young man always comments sarcastingly applying very bitter tone, "Are you intending to re-marry any teenage girl as you are preparing your body and being in the same way as the youngsters do." O! Providence how can a man tolerate such tilitating-natured wife and what can he do in such an atmosphere?" "Although make up, decorations wearing colourful clothes and jewellries' are considered the social previlege of a woman, but what harm will it do, if a prosperous man wears colourful dresses, ornaments and pays proper attention about his artificial charms without preventing his wife. If a man uses talcum, powder, fairness creams, fragrances, various aids, oils lotions and several types of face and body massaging creams. How is he committing offences? And how is he doing any wrong for the civilised society if, the wife of such man objects very deeply and bitterly comments, "God has blunderly mistaken to make you male because you have all instincts of a female" Tell me O! divine powers, how can he love and like such wife?"

"Human nature, mental composition, habitual disposition are framed and blessed by God. There are an abundance of human species of features and women on Earth as serious or grave men passionate or sentimental men, dry and logical introverts, extroverts, funny, humorous, comic, cynical, kind and hard cored persons. There are ever seeming wooed person and ever seeming jolly and jubliant persons. But, there are some persons whose nature is very difficult to understand the inner temperament which flashes like a revolving disc. They change or the nature is automatically getting changed according to the situations and routine confrontations. They laugh, look sad, angry and despondent frequently such men are very angry when something wrong causes his wrath. They laugh wholeheartedly when any jubilation comes. They appear the most dried and unhappy fellows when any trouble comes for their changeful nature, they cannot be declared, blamed or faulty. Suppose such natured man was laughing in his private office at any comic issue among colleagues and staffs including males and females no sooner he reaches his home than any bad news he receives and turns very ferocious through his mental and physical appearance, if inspite of balming and cooling, his wife also competes with him in the same tone, mood and minds, temperament and if she makes a very vulgarly, bitter verbal expression like thus, "There is no fouled mean in the world as you are as you were laughing with your heart roaring in your office before lusty and demoralising sexies and the eternal master of death has caught you while reaching home before me because you appear as if someone has thrusted a sabre into your intestine." O! Tulsi my fair supporter tell me how can gentleman make peace with such wife???"

24

Spontaneity and Validity of Love

Dear "Tulsi", how difficult and impossible to make love with such woman who is filled with gall wholely. Love is the profound passion of human heart, it is only the purest passion which can conquer the fear of death. True love is nicest and unique gift of God to mankind. It is the pivot of life wheel, a guiding star and the everlasting source of making life joyful, interesting and colorful. Shakespeare, the supreme bard has rightly said—

"Things base and vile
Holding no quantity
Love can transpose
Form and dignity"

"A loveful man is the stark optimist, because the universal power of love removes all clouds of pessimism and darkness. True love is an all pervasive and long lasting power. It can vivify even the dead and lifeless objects. Listen and brood carefully on this love lyric!

"True love never echoes
It is deep and dumb
It passes through

Bosom kernal

And makes external plumb

It paves path for dream hopes

Making something, marring something

It keeps infinite scopes in it

Bringing something, sending something

Love life God and nature.

Love duty work and praytor

Love song, and singing singer

Love joy divine bless bringer

Love not slays

Love not blaze

Love not hot

Love not raze.

Love makes

Celestial thought sense

Alters not love

Makes dense

Love measure less

Love number less

Love form Infinite

Figureless

Love teach lover
Love full life
Love preach lover
To rid knife

Love beats not
Love get beaten
Love loads not
Love get loaden

Beauty and wealth
Health, height
Strata, caste
And pride
Love makes not
Distincts not

Love height is untouchable
Love possesses not hearty pebble

No place or
Power wisdom
To confine
True love seldom

Be learned
Wise and seer

To delve deep
Love unpeer

Life in heaven
Is Ever
Who makes to
Life love server

Life is wastage futile
If not makes
It love pile

O! Gentle learaned
And renown
Go read and sense
This love is pun".

Till what extent should I describe about the validity and profoundness of love. It is unfathomably deep love passions are vaster and deeper than sea. But at the same time, love is the most psychological output, mind is the universal storehouse of such feelings. Most modern terms we call it "mood", which is an articulated substitute of mind.

There is a very strange atmosphere of psychological world of any body. First of all, the mind of a man likes or gets attracted towards anything else.

But simultaneously, love is the most spontaneous feeling of human heart. No pressure fear power, attraction or greediness can compel anyone to produce it. So, if an insensible wife forces her husband love her by the dint of marital bond, how can it be possible to do so...????

PART–III

25

World and Its People

This beautiful earth is full of multitude creatures and species of human beings and diversity of natural panoramas. Men live on this Earth in a very different modes "Most men eddy about" i.e., many people walk here and there uselessly and aimlessly. They stand and talk at many places, gossip throughout lives, they neither do well nor make any harm to the world and ultimately they die, mixing in the dust and people forget them just after their deaths. The second type of men are the busiest creature among materialistic tendencies only to hoard money to eat, drink and be merry in their lives and works. In the end, very few remember them for their materialistic achievement. But, there are some whose lives are totally at stake for the welfare of humanity. They do common duties and work but differently from others. Their work and action is the lesson and ideal for others, they possess unique courage indomitable will-power, fervent frenzy for action and superb, noblest thoughts. For them, this whole world is a family and they are the father, saviour and hero of human beings. I have noticed several affinits between good men and doctor Nilay Sir. He was a very, energetic and enthusiastic person.

26

Love for Mother Land

Nilay Sir was a true lover of mother land-an ardent and great worshipper of his country India. He would often say whenever the occasion called and situation forced him speak through such words "Tulsi" "the true service of our motherland is to awake, to educate and to make its people capable, skilled and trained. A nation can be developed only when its citizens become educated rich and cultured." Nilay was often very despondent thinking about the heavily miserable and crucial state of Indian Army on the front with the deep sigh he would say, "If my Indian government and military do not voilet the rules of international peace pact, why do other neighbouring countries commit the brutual act of beheading our men violating international love and brotherhood". He was a worthy substantial potential, action oriented and a worthy, son of his motherland. In order to make genuine service to his motherland sometimes he had pledged having been looked down by some examiners during his P.G. viva examination. Perhaps someone out of the examination body had commented bitterly at his being belonged to very backward and under-developed district. It was the occasion of sir's viva examination of English literature on a Master of Art level. A group of learned examiners was present in a big hall. Candidates were being called one after another. When he was summoned, he faced a very challenging oral examination. Sir was very deeply shocked with the behaviour of some learned professors, who were looking him badly down on being an U. Pian candidate particularly of Brahmapuri and Champawati district. It was sir's strong faith that learning and talents never recognise any particular place or province. They can be anywhere. So, any weak person particular in learning must not be condemned after his region.

Thus, when Nilay Sir confronted those huge wind-mill like persons, he gave a very strong and mouth-breaking reply. The chief examiner asked him "Where do you belong to?" He replied, "I am from Brahmpuri, U.P." He spoke in a very ridiculous manner, "Are there such persons also in Brahmpuri who read so authentic and speak English so fluently".

Sir was so profoundly hurt that he never forgot this event rather he swore raising his sturdy hands towards heaven, "I will never leave my mother land Brahmapuri I will do my utmost best and fullest attempt to make my city progressive." He wanted to remove illiteracy from his land and wanted to fill the place with the true light of knowledge, where he dwelt within a period of ten years. He had opened three educational institutes-two in Brahmpuri and third one in the neighbouring district name Champawati.

27

Champawati School Branch and Madam Sona Kalia

It is very important to delineate about this institution, which was perhaps the root cause of sir's suffering and agony.

It was the shuddering month of December when Nilay Sir purchased a big land for college construction in Champawati district. After making the herculean attempt, Nilay Sir succeeded in raising the needed school building there. During establishment of third college branch, sir was charged with revolutionary courage, energy, power and passion. He was racing against time, he took all challenges faced many risks and put his life several time on stake. He succeeded in maintaining his dream castle which got ready after unnumbered efforts. He managed to equip with the furniture, technical and scientific apparatus very soon; office got ready and became well-furnished. There was an urgent need of some devoted and ably qualified persons to give the institute a starting push and may run with it representing him or herself as a deserving principal. It took six months. The month of June arrived with its ferocious dusty winds accompanied with occasional overshoot of rainfall.

As the educational norm says, "A principal is the most important figure among the academic staff members. He/she dominates the whole institution. He/she overshadows at all the big or small issues of the institution as well as the mode of teaching and working bodies. He/she must be regular, punctual, moral, devoted, hardworking and a person of good character and holy thought. Besides, he/she must be faithful person for the institution and its chair-person as well". So, it was a very complicated selection for which sir had shortlisted many names and ultimately he got fixed with the name of a teacher, who was experience of five years in his own institution as well as, fully devoted. smart and energetic. Her name was Sona Kalia without delay or hindrance, she was called in for the meeting as soon as Nilay sir announced about her promotion. She got charged with indomitable power and infinite courage.

Human nature and mental disposition are made and framed by God. Madam Kalia was wise, educated, trained, experienced, devoted and extremely laborious, but sometimes her nature seemed very funny. She often behaved like a child she prattled and showed stubbornness. Perhaps, she was quiet unaware about the tactics and enticements. She came from low upbringing and was so simple and innocently plain in behaviour that such type of nature and behaviour became a very big drawback or defect with her personality. Simultaneously, she was completely failure in dealing with crook, cynical, cunning men and frauds. She was passing her thirties at the time.

No sooner did Madam Sona Kalia receive the news of her promotion and transfer than she became extremely happy. She paid lot of thanks, good wishes and blessings for Nilay sir in the name of God and the very next morning she actively executed holding of new responsibilities in the third educational institution of Nilay sir. She was frank, bold and an audacious speaker. She handled the seat of principal in the institution as smartly, devotionally, regularly, punctually, truthfully, laboriously and whole hartedly that a desolate place, became enriched and prosperous.

Sir was too happy to be expressed. I asked him "Have your problems got solved, "sir"? How is Madam Sona Kalia holding her responsibilities in the district Champawati. Sir said," O Tulsi! I am very-very happy I found one to whom the institution has needed urgently."

Nilay Sir was in a very jovial mood at the time. He sang a snap of an old movie song—

"Jab Dolti Hai Jeevan ki Nayya
Koi to mil Jata hai Khewaiya".

With it, he began to pour her heart-felt feelings about madam Kalia "I had never thought she would prove herself such skilled principal O! Almighty truely you are the biggest provider, man only proposes. It is certainly that omnipotent, one who disposes everything."

It was the beginning of the second week of heat and moistured June month, when she began to attend her duties. There was a great fuss about this new institute and the new principal madam Sona Kalia altogether in the whole district of Champawati. The days started to roll out very busily within one month. Madam Kalia motivated and convinced more than two thousand guardians. Five hundred wards got there by admitted there in. It provided a good financial aid to sir in a bulk. Nothing kept sir hidden to me. One day he told me," Tulsi! Do you know the state of my new branch? I spent Rupee fifty lakh in establishment and madam Sona had refunded me twenty five lakh within one month." I was overjoyed to listen. How can I not in the happiness of such a *"Mahatma"* who was everything for me my father, guardian, teacher, patron, and true friend? What he did for me none could do. Once I fell badly ill I could not under take any medical treatment due to the emptiness of my purse. Sir had gone out of the state with some important work. On returning, when it came to know about him he furiously persuaded me, Hey! "Tulsi" "You had several leaves of my signed cheques. Why hadn't you withdrawn money from banks for your medical treatment. "Foolish girl"! You don't understand utility and importance of your life and being in my institution. You are my right hand on whom I had enormous trust and on your feminine sturdy shoulders, I have built my mansion of success. If anything goes wrong with you what will happen to me and my school and collages. If you will be healthy, hefty energetic, active, smart and fit, you will keep the institution vice-versa. I will punish you heavily on the next time, if you suffered with any physical ache or sickness and did not take my allowances."

I was mutely listing his epilogue on my suffering. None but I alone could feel the genuine warmth of his passions about me.

So, I wished very hilariously when Nilay Sir broke me out the happy news of his new institution's success.

Days continued to roll away. The good income of the school fulfilled all the required needs. Every thing was going on successfully, but perhaps God's will was indifferent with the success. The work and genuine performance of madam Kalia made her dominant and an aggressive figure in the whole institution. She took all the rights and powers in her own hands so authoritatively that it made some old and senior staff members particularly lady teachers stunned. They began to prejudice vehemently with madam Kalia and uniting all, they began making plots and conspiracy against her. They did their whole attempt for curtailing her powers and authority, but did not succeed; ultimately they decided to put scandalous charges against madam Sona Kalia concerned with Dr. Nilay Sir.

As we have known previously that sir's married life was stagnantly worse, madam Analavati Devi to whom we have known very well was so suspicious and audacious in the matter of throwing sir's unique character out, that a spark, was enough to burn the terrible forest fire. When the lady teaching staff members of Champawati branch have told Analavati, she burnt up with wrath and fury, threatening many disastrous consequences to Nilay sir and madam Kalia.

28

Veneration of Madam Kalia

Madam Sona Kalia was badly industrious. She fulfilled all the duties, responsibilities and necessities very appropriately, except some badly influencing habits. She was sensible enough to understand the learning, greatness, labouriousness and uniqueness of Dr. Nilay sir. So, she fell badly in ideal love with Nilay sir. She adored and honoured him so much that it created a very fatal rumour concerning with her illicit relations with Nilay sir, though the nature of her love for sir is evident in this declaration as once she opened her heart before him, "Listen! "my adorable noble and most loveable person! You know sir my father has died I have heard only about him that he was a very good and laborious person. So, when I see at you, I find my deceased father is standing before me smiling and encouraging." No doubt, Madam Sona Kalia loved Nilay Sir as her father, but it was impossible to make everyone understand about her feelings. She was foolish enough to announce the ideal feelings of love for Nilay sir openly. She would often say, "I love and adore Nilay sir more than anybody else in the world. I can sacrifice my life for him, if he demands."

I have also understood him so deeply and nobly that I have become a lifelong devotee of his virtues. He loves and prefers me to any other person; he cares me very much and fulfills all my required and desired need, as well."

29

Sona Kalia v/s Anala Madam

Madam Sona Kalia did not realise about the tapestries of this cunning and crook world. The prejudiced women staff members started discussing so vulgarly with the certificational quotations of aforesaid Sona's statements that whosoever heard the story regarded the relation of Sona and Nilay Sir illicit and vulgar. Everybody was angry at Madam Sona Kalia. Being a just and dutiful principal, she had punished the guilty teachers. So they conspirated conjointly and the plot got badly successful. They altogether met with Analawati and narrated the fair love story, scandalously breaking all boundaries. Sprinkling extra salt on the burnt finger, they described their mutual treatment, so incestuously by spicing more salt and chilly with sauce that it maddened Analawati. She made universal uproar and full-throated cry with ear-rendering shrieks and announced about the fatal consequences.

After the departure of those conspirators, Anala broke down many useful and costly households as well as fancy articles of drawing room in the fit of her jealousy, anger like a fierce sorceress of any grave yard. She performed more terrible acts, abusing and cursing obscenely she began to wait for Nilay sir's advent. Nearly at 10'O clock in the evening night Nilay sir returned elated with happy mood. As soon as Anala saw him, she caught hold of his shirt collar and made most agonising obscene and dirty reception.

Nilay sir was all stunned, though it was his daily welcome but today's offering was more pungent and severe than other days. He tried his best to convince her, but she was more fierce than roaring river Ghagra both are unstoppable. The day was only for filthy scandalous attacks upon his character, morality and conduct. She abused so vulgarly and threatened so profoundly that sir left home that night secretly and spent the whole night weeping profusely.

The night was very troublesome for me. I was writhing on my bed and was unable to understand about my restlessness. Sir bemoaned, lamented so poignantly that it made the whole nature perturbed that night. His poetic heart shrouded in such elegiac lyrics that night which I found on a paper on his desktop of the head branch.The poem which Sir composed that night runs thus—

O! God Not so, not so, not so.

She says I am a debauchee

They claim I am a faulter

O! God not so, not so, not so.

I Neither Love nor Like her.

So, they say I am a corrupt crook.

But in holy sense genuinely

Not so, not so, not so.

I look others with love and honour

So they say, "I am a mean"

I have a lusty nature

I have a crooked character
But in true senses
O! God not so, not so, not so.
We do much quarrel with one another probably
We fought with one another, sometimes badly
We abused one another often bitterly and vulgarly

We gave one another many woes
We must be beaten with many dirty shoes
Punish me as much as you can
O! Divine but everyone considers
me a villain
O! God not so, not so, not so.
I was fickle, innocent laughable
She filled my heart with malicious pebble
She transformed me
From
Man to brute
Innocent to crook
Sane to lunatic
and a heinous sinner
But in true senses
Not so, not so, not so.

30

Nilay Sir's Agony

The night rolled away with panic and fear when early in the morning, I did not listen any movement of sir's dawn routine. I feebly asked Anala Madam to sir's whereabout. Her bitterest tone realised the meaning of last perturbed night she said, "Somewhere will be dying the wicked unfortunate. God knows where he is? sucking the foulagea outlets of Sona perilous prostitute."

I got ready briskly to reach the institution so that I may get news of my patron's presence, my clouded heart stumbled and stopped to see him lying on a wooden plank of the ground floors' hostel corridor. Casting my fear of feminine honour and Anala's fiery behaviour, I reached him, giving a gentle shake on his forehead I questioned as soon as he opened his eyes, "How are you sir? Why are you lying on this lonely plank? Why haven't you come home? Where have you taken food? Your face is downcast? You look supinely tired. What a picture have you made of yourself? Your galled eyes red orbs sleepy eyelids and severely perturbed mood witness that you have faced any crucial calamity in the night."

Sir did not answer to any of my question. Only his appearance got completely changed listenning my shower of questions. With overflowing tears he only sang the intro of an old song—

"Hathon ki chand Lakiron ka
Ye khel Hai Bus Takdiron ka"

31

Blood-Stained Nuptial Life

There was no need to express anything as my true devotion and adoring sense had told me everything. He exclaimed," O! My father it's too late for me."

Sir started for his home while departing he said, "Tulsi you have to wait in my office after schools-hour in the evening. I have thorny problems to discuss with you."

I got impatient, waited throughout the day for evening college leave, when everybody went away. The doorkeeper came to me bringing his news of my calling, without harming a second. I rushed to his office. The scene of his counter table was also unconvincing as soon as he saw my deeply sympathised face he burst into loud roaring. Generally, sir did not like weeping, nor he was an easy weeper. He would often say "O! diligent persons of my institution never weep at any troubles both adversity and prosperity are the gifts of God. By weeping, we violate and envy the divine being. Life is the name of challenges, trouble and misery. Suffering makes man strong. Tragedies and shocks are the chief weapons of devils making man the adversary to God as mostly people weep and curse God encountring any tragic event."

Sir hated those persons who began to weep very easily. According to him, "challenges are forbearing and are meant for facing not for weeping."

But today, he seemed as tortured and soul panting victim that he couldn't check his forced and agonising tears. He spoke nearly ten minutes after his heart stumbled lamenting "Tell me, Tulsi!, How should I stay alive I am forced to leave my house. I have left all the hopes of amendments. Why does she prejudice so much with me? Are the wives like such? I do not deny about the quarrels between every couple, but such bloody conflicts are rare. You know, "Tulsi" she is now upto destroying my character, prestige and social honour, Tulsi. I persuaded her in many thousand ways but, now I am surrendered and defeated. She shall not improve Tulsi e e e e e e e............ she shall not improve. She says, "I love you. I cannot leave your company, I will not divorce you"

But she does not make a trivial support foregoing our life happily on. The problem is not any one, it is uncountable. She does not like my habits, physical, mental traits and features, my dress sense, my mode of smarting myself, my garnitures, my popularity, fame etc.

Anala bitterly hates my parents, brothers and sisters. She often puts obnoxious and scandalous charges upon my generation, dynasty, race and birth place. She does not leave even my native districts but abuse ferociously. She condemns my family rituals, deities and traditions proving that they are foolish and foul. She had drawn a very strong line of conflict between two different regions of eastern and western U.P. She abhors the person who loves and likes me. She disdains with the invitations which call me specially. She burns up with extreme fury if someone praises my dress, physique, look, hairs, movement and tacts of fitness. She never likes my shopping or any articles brought from the market. She suspects at every word and act she even does not like my camera-drawn photographs, if they are smart and good looking. She may kill if possible, the person, particularly feminine ones, if they shoot any photo with me. She badly suffers from damaging inferiority complex which has maddened her, snatched her virtues and made her away as ruthless as 'Lady Macbath' in Shakespeare's famous tragedy, "Macbeth". O! Tulsi Gods are also not assisting me in this predicament. Can they not transform her heart and mind? "She often said, "I love you very much."

"But paradoxically, she does not care about my meal and breakfast, my bed or body. Only as a lusty ghost, she assaults upon me for surfeiting her sexual urges. Is it the holy bond of marriage? Or are *Ardhanginis* like such? She is quiet unacquainted about my impulsive nature, passionate heart, thoughtful behaviour and philosophical mind. If I make any uproar, she heavily, terribly and bitterly blackmails me. Due to the fear of my prestige and honour, I bear the pain and brunt smilingly. She threatens to kill herself to destroy me totally what can I do Tulsi? How should I live Tulsi? Speak!. Don't stand like statue I do not want to die. Life is the superb gift of God that must not be destroyed at any rate. "To be or not to be was the problem of Hamlet "The Prince of Denmark, but I cannot think about dying because "Canon goes gainst self-slaughter, O! God.. God!".

"If I re-marry she says that she will neither live nor let others live happily. Hindu marriage law is also bitterly adverse for me. Then what? How? and where should I go?

She appears always happy and contented. No sooner I confront her, she turns excessively choleric and allergic. I do not want to commit suicide. Committing suicide is the most cowardice sin which can never be excused even by God."

32

Desire to Convert Religion

"Tulsi", though I love, honour my religion much, which is surely an excellent and glorious one. I have very unshakeable and profound faith in all deities chiefly *'Maha Dev'* who inspite of being supreme owner of all universal owners is called. *'Bhole Nath'* i.e., a very innocent divine master. As well as in *Brahma, Vishnu, Maa Jagdamba* and I am a very fond fan of *'Natwar Girdhar' Bansiwale Krishna Kanhaiya,* yet many times a thought of converting myself into Muslim came. Tulsi, I will change my religion and will be a Muslim to rid off from over-possesive sheepish-behaved wife Anala by marrying twice with any simple-natured girl of any poor family so that I may live in peace. It is too! too! too! much for me. My heart shall burst my head will hameorrhage and I will die in harness that I never want. I would have died perhaps many years ago, if the virtuous acts and good deeds of my parents had not booned and sustained me. Perhaps, providence wants me to retain alive and energetic, but her severest foul behaviour made me psychologically disturbed and neurotic. Tulsi, now I feel giddy motions while ascending and descending stair case of the building. I cannot tolerate the downward looking from a high point. I get easily and immediately annoyed. I have become intemperate and constitutionally feeble. It has also affected my eyesight. I suffer from dyspepsia. O! My God! How should I survive?"

With these confessions, sir got temporarily relieved from overpowering tensions but could not resist his tragic emotions. Shedding tears unceasingly from his blood-red eyes, he continued staying into his private office room and went on narrating his woeful tale. "How should I tell you, 'Tulsi! How much wantonly clever happy and a melodious singer I was in my childhood. Everybody knows I hardly had completed studies of my tenth standard and was not more than fourteen years of age when I happily proposed Anala and requested my relatives and parents to assist me in marrying with her.

"When I met with her firstly she seemed very coy, innocent, delicate, cultured and extremely beautiful. I commemorate the day Tulsi when I kept my forehead on the *Shivalinga* of my domestic temple and implored very earnestly with the Lord *Shiva* to unite me with Analawati Devi. How should I revel now about my opposition as it was my own selection. O! brother of poor saviour of innocents! O! universal proprietor of tri-world and fourteen mansions, incarnate before help me, guide and tell me the way what should I do and where should I go...?"

With these elegiac revelation, sir got swoon. I was in a state of very sorrowful dilemma, I shook his shoulders being badly perturbed and shocked thinking what had happened with him. I began to cry, many members of the college family and staff gathered over there. Doctors were called in. He was provided best medical assistance, sir was sent home.

Many days rolled away. Sir, neither looked normal nor attended to his duties. Every person of his vast empire was more affected due to his absence for two weeks but he did not come to his headquarter. On the Monday of the third week, he came very stealthily as he was shuddering in his own institution.

Perhaps, he was badly shocked hearing about his fainting, as he always opposed frailty. Shubhra Madam, the principal of his prime institution came and asked about his well messages. She politely requested him to come for the morning assembly to address students with his speeches of nobility and gentility. As soon as Nilay sir heard her request, he turned very somber and began to recite a poem smilingly and ironically—

"How can I preach about nobility and gentility
While I myself great guilty
So don't call me gentle.
I am no more this.

I taught others
Morality, conduct and character
The path of nobility
Greatness and sanity
Now I am myself
a great guilty.
My mind, wisdom
Intellect and discreete
All could not prevent
to be called me a hypocrite
Elederly were ever stunned.
To see my purity and mind bent
In my region, I was honoured as a sage
I was popular among English page

Now I am a foul preacher
Perhaps, a most blunderring creature
Now, I have no goodness chart
How can I unveil my heart?"

We were all very sorry listening to his innocent confession we sought very humbly. Sir came forth the assembly and addressed them with his mighty and noblest speech.

I remained very grieved after the office episode. I visited many temples and took an oath to visit every Monday to *Sansari Mata* temple, situated on the way to head campus on the bank of a narrow *'Sarayu'* stream. But, Anala madam was quite unintelligible about sir's agony. There was no change in her ruthless and rude behaviour rather she became more ferocious in her behaviour after conversing with Champawati college branch conjuring ladies-staff. She encountered several times with Madam Sona Kalia. After listening the stealthy complaints of prejudicing ladies-staffs of Champawati branch. Anala madam very disdainfully abused and insulted Madam Kalia warning her not to behave foolishly with Nilay sir.

Fortune worked against the trio to Madam Sona Kalia, to Champawati college branch and to Dr. Nilay sir. It made Sona Madam insane temporarily. She forgot all feminine banns. She perhaps was bewildered to see the glamour of money, position and honour. No doubt, the power and authority had dismayed her as she started expressing publicly her feelings of affection among the college retinue.

She said, "I am born for Nilay Sir. He is everything for me my friend, guardian and my own. When I look at him, I find the resemblance of my father and my God both in him. I can live and die several times for him."

Madam Sona Kalia had become over-spontaneous. It had led her astray to some extent. Though, she would say openly that she was a dedicated devotee of Nilay sir and so her all feelings were for him. Simultaneously, she talked very closely, passionately and affectionately with few rich guardians and some male college staff members. No doubt her fickle and flirting behaviour had created a lot of rumour around Nilay sir's institutions. Sir has attempted his best to improve her childishly wrong behaviour, but the dominant fate had blinded her. On several occassions, sir attempted his best to instill in her the good virtues of nice conduct, character and morality. But whenever sir parsuaded her, she pretended as if she knew everything and did not value the precious suggestions of uniquely learned and great man. Her frequent calls on several persons' cell phone was a very foolish act. Though, she did not want to make anything wrong for the institution, but she could not help to maintain the honour and prestige. She was nearing her thirties, but was foolish enough like a teenage girl in few matters. Her dress sense was also very awkaward. She often wore gorgeous clothes with dense and glittering embroidery. Despite many objections by Nilay sir and few other well-wishing person of the institution, she did not improve. She put on the dresses like actresses in dancing scenes during any modern film shooting. Besides, her darkly red, green and yellow clothes, her sense of facial make up was worth opposing. She was unmarried, but she applied bright red lipsticks on her lips and rosy talc on her cheeks with shining particles of cosmetics. No gentle person had ever liked her apparel and decorations. It demoralised the college atmosphere because the novice teachers were following the silhouette of their principal madam Sona Kalia. The prejudicing women teachers were not silent they were creating much scandal about Madam Kalia that was annoying and appalling Anala Madam much. She was doing bloody conflicts everyday with

Nilay sir, charging more dirty and heineous blames on his character and chastity with unmindful obscenity.

One day having found sir lonely in the college library, I couldn't resist my query with courage and humble tone, I questioned sir, mentioning the scandalous charges with Kalia madam I found the answer to my questions without any objection. He said, "Why not Tulsi; may I not fall up to such depravity I may be debauchee, if you believe so?." I was bent with shame and realisation of self-guilt. My question did not affect him. He was as cool and calm as he was before making this query. A context from *Aranya Kand* from the *Radhey Shyam Ramayan* turned alive before me when Maricha, the disguised devil as deer roamed away before Lord *Rama* and without shriek calling upon the name of *Laxman* when he got struck with lord Rama's arrow. Sita urged *Laxman* to seek Rama to help him as she suspected some impending trouble with him. *Laxman* then said—

"Bole tab shri lakhan ji

Mata dhariye dheer

Dukkha kahan jab dukkha ke

Nashak hain Raghubeer

Kiska sahas hain He Mata

Jo unhe dukkha pahuchayega

Suraj jis jagah prakashit ho

Kab waha andhera chhayega"

Goddess Sita had indirectly accused Laxman for being selfish in coming to the forest with Rama. She spoke—

"Boli Sita main jan gayi
Matlab ka bhaichara hai

Ghar se jo tum van aaye ho
Isme kuchha swarth
Tumhara hai"

Mother Sita had charged Laxman with the blames of selfishness. Laxman was neither disturbed nor affected with Sita's undue charges. The reaction was natural—

"Bachan nahi yeh vajrasa saman
Gira lakhan par ek
Ruen-Ruen se toot kar
Tukde bane anek"

But it made no long effect on Laxman—

"Kshada bhar tak bhi
In bato ka
Laxman ji par
Na prabhav raha
Wo nirmal nishkalanka
Sewak
Waise hi aaral swabhav raha"

I faced while questioning Dr. Nilay sir scandalous charges concerned with Madam Sona Kalia. Few more days rolled away but there was no improvement in the nature, behaviour and dress sense of madam Kalia. Nearly everybody in the college campus turned hostile. Some were praying deities for her annihilation, though she was foe to none. She had no prejudice nor malice for anybody else. She was very kind to those who would often disburse her brought food to others and remained hungry throughout the day. The most damaging foolery what she demonstrated was her daring declaration of devotional feelings and affectional sentiments for Nilay sir. As we have been well acquainted with the fact that the religious wife of Nilay sir was so bitter in this matter that she could not tolerate the shadow of any woman upon Nilay sir. So, these scandals about which madam Kalia was not motived any least, burnt the entire peace and sanity of Anala's mind. For giving strong lessons to Sona, Anala Ma'm began to reach the institute suddenly and on every visit she insulted and thrashed her badly. A crucial conflict broke between Anala and Sona Ma'm's, which would often influence others. It was the first, national festival day in the college. I was also instructed by sir to attend the function of the new college branch at Champawati, perhaps during rainy season. Madam Sona Kalia was very happy to receive two hundred staff members. She was busily rushing here and there for preparing the event as many students were going to perform dance on some patriotic song. Madam Kalia was herself the director of that musical ballad. It was midday. Thousand of people gathered therein across the well equipped and decorated auditorium. The stage was ready Mr. P.K. Banerjee the vice-principal of the school was announcing showering great praise on the students' effort as well as college arrangement. Everybody was happy and was eagerly waiting for the start of cultural programme. Nearly everybody wore and ornaments according to the occasion, only Sona madam was looking very eerie in her appearance. She was running here and there briskly wherever she went, she called upon Nilay sir for advice and help. Anala could not bear with her frequent approach. She was furious. The oversmart and wanton behaviour of madam Kalia infuriated her, she stopped her in a room and said, "Nonsense woman! why do you frequent my husband? Can you not inquire the problems at once? Who are you to be so close with him? Are you his keep-basterd? Madam Kalia could not hold her mind. She screamed "Ye-e.e.e.sh! I am his everything............Have you heard? ....What wrong can you make about me?" It was too much for the gracious madam Analawati Devi to tolerate. She got maddened. Though, she was very angry, yet she ordered madam Kalia in very effective threatening words, "Leave my institute immediately. There is no need of such whore in this pious institution. I dismiss you forever this is the total punishment for you". Sona madam at once lifted her handbag and rushed out covering her face with a handkerchief, shedding silent tears. Nobody checked her only the door keeper followed her and enabled one vehicle to her reach home. It was the end of Sona's episode in Nilay sir's college as principal. Sona madam belonged to a very poor family. Her education and upbringing had been very poor. She was chronic patient of lungs infection which could never be treated medically owing to lack of money. She would periodically fall ill. The doctors had warned her to be careful about her health. She never heeded at the physician's advice. She neither cured herself well nor ever completed the course of medicines properly. There was a rumour that she had been suffering from tuberculosis for over a year but madam Sona Kalia remained fit and well after leaving the Champawati school branch. After one year she fell ill very badly and died in the hospital. Though, she never returned to the institution, several principals came but couldnot fill the void of her dutifulness and dedication. When Nilay sir heard the sad news of her death, he was extremely sorrow but nobody could stop the cruel destiny as somebody has said, "What is lotted cannever be blotted."

33

Predicament that befell !

As we know, "Time and tide wait for none." Days continued to roll away. The time has healed up many wounds. It has made several injuries. The sad demise of Sona madam also gave a strong message that one must not take one's disease carelessly. Perhaps, the age old saying is well meaningful. It is *"Har Insan Ko karz, Farz, aur Marz kabhi Nahi Bhoolna Chahiye"*. The saying reveals that disease, duty and debt must be remembered daily. They must be cured and paid carefully. Madam Sona Kalia who inspite of being highly educated, was completely careless about her chronic illness that resulted into her pre-mature death. Though time was passing fast but the speedy passage of time did not bring any solace in the loathsome behaviour of Analawati Devi, rather she grew more bitter, agressive and dominant in her words, behaviour and treatment with Nilay sir, who was perhaps the predestined prey of Devi ji.

Although, there was no change in Anala Madam but quiet contrary, Nilay sir got completely changed. There was no lustre, smartness and electrical appeal left in his personality. He had become very low-tempered, weak and quarrelsome. The small things could annoy him badly. He began to suffer from insomnia.

He had become irregular, unpunctual and routineless in work and duty. Very few noticed this change, because mostly people came and did their duties, returned home with any awareness of sir's get-well messages.

I was too sorrowful seeing this condition of the person, who was bad to none and was good for everything. I decided to meet and talk with sir about his hodge-podge behaviour. He began to reach office in very late hours. One day, when I could not tolerate this mysterious sorrow I blurted out O! sir, "What has happened with you? Has something gone wrong? In what way do you manage your work?You have got completely changed sir. I am not looking that hard workoholic and smart, regularly punctual fellow whom I have been continuing to see during previous days. Sir, you are the most ideal guide that ammends other imperfections. If you go wrong, everything will destroy automatically. You are not taking your meals and breakfast timely and properly. You are turning weaker day by day. Are you knowingly ruining yourself?." I had a very questioning nature. I posed many questions, but he was no more affected with my interrogation. Rather he said, "Tulsi, I don't have any fear about my ruin or death, because they are no more furious than the life which I face everyday over night and day." With this expression, he began to chant this elegiac lyric—

"Now, I don't fear death

I have tasted many hundred times

With full depth

It may be big bug

For those, who are unaware

For me, a simple fool

Death is not my killer

It will be my saviour

In the End

Death often attacks

Upon me with full blow

It penetrates my soul

And renders my psyche

Slow-n-slow

It is fugitive

In the day

But Gallant

In the absence of light

It has bemoaned

And bewailed me

For severaal nights

It has got caught

Me so bitterly

It has pealed

My bark so severly

I remained smiling

I could not quench my boiling

It made me

A prophet, a seer

It brought bloody, tears

It made me sleep

With open eyelids
It made crimson
To my eyepits
But I was ever
A fighter
So fought with
Anguish slighter
It tormented
My being
It clouded
My seeing
But could not kill me.
See! I am alive.
Even today
With a fresh thrive"

PART–IV

34

The Sweet Dream

I was a mute listener before sir's philosophical utterances, although I could not sense the meaning but one thing did I surely knew that sir was speaking in a state of extreme anguish. As sorrow was evident on his face and divine dew-drops were innerly shining in his celestial eyes. I could not hold myself normally rather I began to sob in his feelings evident of deep sorrow. Sir did not remain there with tragic feeling. He went away. I remained thinking about his tragic life more deeply than previous speculation. One thing was very satisfying about his nature that was his changeful mood. No sorrow or suffering could force him sad for a long time. Perhaps, he has quiet mastered in triumphing over miserable situations. No doubt, his temperament was a revolving disc, which changed nearly after every three or four hours. It soothed me very much as I saw him smiling and laughing at every changed moment.

Nearly a quarter of century had passed to the marriage of Dr. Nilay sir with madam Analawati Devi. Nearly twenty years would have certainly gone since I was working in his institution, residing at his own house. If I should try to recall the past and gone reminiscences. I can hardly recollect any week when very soul-stirring verbal duel that did not occur. I was much troubled with the estrangment. Sir had been so accustomed to her reception that he had adapted to such an atmosphere.

He would often say—

"Ab nahi taklif deti hain

Mujhe rushwaiyan

Zakhmi dil itne dino se hai

Ki aadat ban gayi"

But in true senses, there is none in the whole world who does not like love, joy, happiness and pleasures of the world. Pretences may be one thing but true suffering is very hard to tolerate. Sir was not an exception to this rule.

"Dear readers"now I am going to narrate avery loving story. Once, I listened such a heart smashing pathetic tale of sir's vision that I could never forget. Once when sir had some easy moments, he came to me. It was the finishing month of December with benumbing cold and said, "O! Tulsi, I want to narrate a very joyful dream, which I have seen last night, "Lord Shiva incarnated before me and said, "O! Dr. Nilay your days of suffering have finished, they will be no more as I am transforming your being. Just after my disappearance, you will be a quite changed man with a fresh and new life and with most virtuous, beautiful and gracious new wife as you have dreamt several times to have. I am omniscient, I have known your pent up desires. Consequently, I have reunited you with your dream lady". With this *Bhole Nath* has disappeared. Truely after His departure, I found my sole self to have completely changed. The lady with whom Lord Shiva had united, was truely an ideal and the most virtuous woman. Who was ready to follow and admit my wishes? She was agreed with me totally she said to me, "I am fortunate enough to be your companion and sharer of your woes and happiness. You don't know about your's own greatness, nobility, learning and uniqueness of your heart. The virtues of my many lives have assembled altogether and made me your wife." "Tulsi"! "She was truely the outcome of my past wish-model of imagination. She ordered me with firm tone of love, "Listen! "Mr. Doctor" You are very careless about your health and security" showing me a chart she said, "This is your meal and diet chart breakfast at 7:30 with the good ingredients of nutritious menu involving fruits, fats and sweets. Lunch at 12:30 with completely balanced dishes of Indian kitchens, dinner at 7:30 with light food involving some snacks chapattis and pulses."

"I swayed with joy. My soul was leaping with happiness and heart was dancing with her affection. All of a sudden, she caught hold my hand and took me into the house, dragging affectionately and said, "This is your wardrobe with party wears on the left side and right side wardrobe is full of daily wearing clothes. I had made the maid to arrange your shoes and slippers in this rack so that you may find them when you need. She had shown my clean, nice, fragrant and light bedroom, annexed with nice drawing room for guests aside. I was overwhelmed with love, pity and joy to see the well maintained kitchen and hygienic toilet. In the end, she said?" Listen, my dear! carefully I will never leave you alone particularly during meals while shopping or going to the house of any relative during auspicious ceremony and on the bed time. You will not cry for servants and maid for drinking water, lifting your coat and providing you articles of daily preparation. I was in the seventh heaven, in the mean time my eyes opened hearing some rustling noise on my front door. I found my personal attendant knocking for some cash urgently needed for the vehicles, fuel at 5:30 am. The pleasure and contentment which I felt during this soothing sweet dream was indescribable O! for such days perhaps, they might be real! How good it were!".

Nilay sir was looking very pitiable and full of over impulsiveness. I reacted very fickle-mooded to change him by interrupting with narration of some day-to-day affairs, which brought dramatic relief–in him and me.

35

The Confession before In-law Members

Days were passing very fastly. The change of time ushered in several changes in Nilay sir's institution and behaviour. Sir was attempting his best to bring harmony in his family life. He went on picnics and tours frequently to many places to bring some change in Anala's behaviour. He surrendered his will and ambition before her. Sir told her about his many ambition and enterprising plans, what he was going to undertake in the coming time. He also described about his future dream, but Anala did not receive or notice them happily rather she jeered that it could make him merry. No tour visit or picnic delighted her rather she continued commenting on the shortcoming or trouble due to the journey and continued killing the joyful soul of pleasant journey. Nearly a year passed in these curative attempts of Dr. Nilay sir, but all attempts have turned in vain, as there was neither any control at her malicious tongue nor she ever did any effort to bring peace, harmony and compromise in their conjugate life. Sir was badly perturbed with failed attempts as some audacious persons out of his staff began to criticise about his disgusting state of cohabitation.

Sir was badly helpless on his failures, as many people had questioned him why was he not able to harmonise his family relation. One day by chance nearly all the members of Anala's parents house reached to meet her. Nilay sir thought that he should tell about his suffering to them with the expectation that perhaps they might help in some way to extinguish this constant burning hearth. So, he called for a meeting inviting his father-in-law, mother-in-law, brother-in-law and wives of his brothers-in-law. When everybody sat on their respective places, sir addressed them, "O! My respected uncle aunty and dear brothers-in-law! "Listen carefully, you know that God has given me much prosperity and wealth, so I am happy and leading a joyful life, now, the truth is not like this. I kept my mouth shut for twenty five years, during these years I have transformed myself into a man of the world from a novice, become grave from fickle and professional, have sons and daughters. But, no time gave us any peace or happiness with my wife—I mean with the lady, who is your daughter. You know gentlemen! "We have been constantly quarreling sometimes fighting with one another for these long past years. The inclinations are multitude and cannot be described. Every situation and nearly each matter of talk creates disharmony which results into fierce duel and sometimes we strike our hands mutually. Nobody can think so, nobody can believe so, nobody can guess so but it is true. We are never at peace. So, today I have opened my heart among you for redressal. My parents have died, brothers have parted. They don't have any concern about my misery, but you all are alive, healthy and wise. I request you earnestly with my composed hand and bent head. Beseech you must do something which outshine our beings."

After this confession, sir went to his work house. He did not like to waste a single moment of time. All the members of sir's in-law house remained glued with awe. They asked about this disconcord to Anala Ma'm as the above expression shows that sir had not described his disputed state clearly rather he had given only an indirect hint of his quarrelsome life. He neither told about his own faults nor to Ma'm Analwati, so they understood the conflict, but none of them knew about the cause. Anala's real mother i.e., the real mother-in-law of Dr. Nilay sir had died long ago, when she was child. Analawati had step-mother and step-brother. Only sir's father-in-law Mr Jagdeesh Prasad was really associated with the blood relations to Analawati Devi; so when the disclosure about his daughter's bridal stage came, the brothers along with mother and wives made a strong oppose and created a bitter contempt for Dr. Nilay sir. They began to ask about the cause of such crucial inclinations. Although Analawati's behaviour about Nilay sir was very contemptuous and bitter. She had never told about this state of life to her parents and brothers. She was also stunned listening to sir's confession. In the absence of Nilay sir, she found very appropriate chance to excite and goad her family members. She put several charges, uncompensationable and very foul estimation of debauchery and lustfulness. She claimed that success, wealth and prosperity had blinded Nilay sir. Consequently, he had begun to behave like a complete licentious person. She convinced them so properly that they accepted the undue charges about his licentiousness. I do not know the reasons, but it was quiet clear that Nilay sir did not like the persons of his in-law's house—his father-in-law, as well his step mother-in-law and his brothers-in-law. Perhaps, in the beginning of his career, when Nilay sir was a sufferer and struggler, none of them had ever supported or cooperated rather they mocked at his destiny obscured and jeered at his short and simple annals and way of his living.

The time had taught Nilay sir. Those things which he did not possess in his early career. So many times he had very disgustfully been insulted by them at their own house. Thus, he had changed himself completely from their sides. None of them had any real honour or affection for Nilay sir due to emotion and mind afflicting tensions. Nilay sir had spoken unfavourably about them so the relation between Nilay sir and them was not satisfactory. It was the benovelence of almighty God that clustered sir with many successes and prosperities that shut their mouth forcibly. The whole city honoured him and he was famous for and wide for his honesty, truthfulness and as a man of the words, labour and gentality:

The eldest brother-in-law of Nilay sir was so badly furious that he challenged him for his downfall and destruction. He never remained happy with Nilay sir due to some differences of nature and habits. Over all, Nilay sir's confession among the persons of his in-law house did not turn out fruitful rather it angered his the in-laws bitterly. The most damaging influence of this confession was the downfall of Nilay sir's image and prestige in the view of his in-laws. Now, they also began to talk obscenely about his name and character only the father in law of Nilay sir got badly upset listening to this exposure as he considered that his daughter along with son-in-law was living very happily.

36

Taking Legal Refuge

The confession created more problems in Nilay sir's life. Now, the hidden matter became apparent. His brothers-in-law, their wives and his step mother-in-law stood among the relatives and friends responsible for, Sir's sullen image and prestige everywhere Because Anala had blamed him for his illicit relations with madam Sona Kalia. Now, the state of sir's survival became more difficult and thorny. Its misfortunes did not kneel down. He was still attempting to improve his family woes. His confession was one of the efforts to make them convinced about the disharmony thinking perhaps they might parsuade her not to misbehave.

Few more days passed. Sir had consulted with several people who were claiming to be his well-wishers, but they only tasted better as joy but did nothing. Nilay sir had a legal advisor, who was law practitioner in the high court namely Kamla Kant Srivastava. Sir called him for the private meeting. On his arrival sir gave him a very warm welcome and sat in his private chamber of the head branch. Sir had narrated the woeful tale of his personal life. Kamlakant was bewildered at the suffering of such man to whom he would say among his sons and daughters, as truthful and dutiful as "Harishchandra"the king of Indian mythology and hard-working as a bull. Kamlakant knew Nilay sir since his career. His sons and daughters took private tuition in English language and grammar for many years. They all were highly successful due to the superb knowledge and understanding of English language imparted by Dr. Nilay sir in his coaching centre. Without thinking ahed, he at once said, "Sir you must divorce her. She is not your wife. She is an enemy of your past life. If she thus behaves as you have said I am preparing the papers. I will file a suit of divorce against her." Hearing the word 'divorce' sir became extremely disturbed. He asked "What ground will you show for divorce?." Kamlakant replied "I have several grounds that she is a woman of very loose character, completely careless about her duties as committed wife, abuses you publicly and keeps illicit relation with many people. She is very cruel to her husband". Interrupting in the middle, sir exclaimed. O! No she is not like this. Her character is no way foul. She had only a very bitter sense of inferiority complex that underrates herself, being so bitter. She suffers from the melody of regionalism and provincialsm. Her extraordinary sense of superiority being the product of eastern part of the state has made her foolish and ridiculous. She tries to speak several English words, while she cannot speak Hindi, her mother tongue well. She suffers from doubts and disobedience. Her love is only a show, not real ones. Her passions and sentiments are completely artificial. She does not have any interest in my health, fitness, power and success. Sometimes, if she pretends before someone else to do her duties, they are only formalities. She never likes my touring, shopping, bringing new clothes and dressing smartly. She envies with all my family members including my deceased parents, brothers and sisters. She jeers at my routine and entertainment. She cannot tolerate to see me physically and mentally healthy. She is burnt with fury, if any lady admires me. Such types of evils she practice daily but she is not debauchee. So sir how can I charge with this filthy blame?."

The barrister Kamlakant Srivastava turned serious and said "If you want to divorce her you have to provide strong grounds besides the ground of cruelity otherwise justice will always be in her favour." Nilay sir said, "I cannot demoralise her, as she has been and is my wife in the view of general public. Can I not run elsewhere farther and re-marry with any other ordinary woman, who can live with peace." "You shall bear penal punishment if you re-marry without divorce and spend your life behind the iron rods." said Kamlakant. Nilay sir futher said, "May it not happen Kamal ji that my stable and unstable property be given to Analawati and make me relieved according to my own will marrying with next one by law. Actually, I don't like to frequent with the court and legal process. Simultaneously, I do not like to make the image of mine and hers dirty and insulting by levying foul charges as everybody of the court nearly all the lawyers, barristers and judges know me well. I have taught the issues of relevance to several jury men." Having heard this emotional lecture of innoncence and morality, Kamlakant Srivastava the barrister began to laugh at his assertion. Ultimately, he spoke. "You are behaving childish sir. Law does not know reputation and honour. These are the essential things which the law never sense. Our legal system urges for strong grounds for the dismissal of any marriage or pact. The legal system lacks from human insight. It does not have passion or sentiment. The law suit is a parade of criss-cross mutually skin-sprinkling the mud. Perhaps, it is the reason why many prestigious families do not file suits in the hidden sexual crimes of their family women. Honour killing is the outcome of the criss-cross laws. When the people get disillusioned with the law, they take it in their own hands and commit crimes." The meeting was interrupted with the arrival of some guadians to Nilay sir's office. Kamlakant Srivastava left the spot, thinking ridiculously about the destiny of Dr. Nilay sir.

37

Brutal Conflict

Madam Analawati Devi was a woman of extremely aggressive when she turned furious. She played havoc in the house by smashing precious articles, breaking costly households, making everything at sixes and sevens, crying with her full- pitch throat. Nothing could stop her. One thing was very worse that fit of her strong anger would always strike either on Nilay sir or some household, if he is absent when she could hurt herself badly. There were unnumbered nail scratches and teeth bites on Nilay sir's whole body particularly on the hand, neck and face that fiercely angered Nilay sir also but being a man of infinite tolerance he kept everything concealed.

38

Act of Vengeance

The clock was running at its proper speed without any break. Seconds were changing into minutes. Minutes into hours. Hours were making days and so on. In the same way, days with weeks and weeks with months, were passing away. New horizon was bringing new aspirations. New aspirations were creating new challenges for Dr. Nilay sir. Despite being very tense and disturbed in personal life, sir was never sitting silently with composed hands and bent head rather he was progressing very fast. He was purchasing new lands, contracting new buildings and planning for newer colleges. He was racing forth with the time and was completing his task before hand, achieving what he had willed.

Sir made up his mind to be ever busy in his institutions so that no time could provoke him to quarrel with Analawati. As she never liked any purchase by Nilay sir from the local market or any distant city, sir had allowed his chief accountant to provide her the needed money whenever she demanded. Thus, Nilay sir did not buy or bring household or any article for his home or for wife. She had a lot of grudge for them. Inspite of having many people, attendants and servants in the late evening Analawati started quarreling with Nilay sir referring any absent that he did not manage. As I had told you O! Humble, gentle and balanced minded readers of the world! That No very special reason caused conflict often a very trivial offense or any little mistake could incite her to provoke a lot of hue and cry. Once, it was the month of April 'The cruelest one' as it is the most joyful month of spring season. According to the period, the college session for the month was very important. Sir was enormously busy in equipping his institutions by advertising and releasing pamphlet. It is the time when the college directors become busy persons. Being a man of indomitable will-power and vaulting ambition. Sir was always thundering in his work house. Analawati was was rudely cunning. She could not let such opportunities go without disturbing. During months of April and July, sir remained so busy that he never took his meal timely and properly. Once he said to me, "Tulsi, April and July are very important months for public school runners. What we sow, we shall reap throughout the year. If somebody beats me with a *lathi* on my back, I do not have time to retaliate. I will go away taking it my as alotted hurt. I do not want any ommission, because it is some sort of comission."

During sir's over busy periods, Anala disturbed him much claiming so many wrong, done in her favour, though the sterling angel did not have time for eating and dressing. How will he offend others? In order to bring more chaos, Anala made a plan for taking poison, so that strong foul rumour might be created and his mission got shattered in the middle of its apex. Under pressure of this ill-will and foul plan, she bought home the rat poison and took a very small amount into her mouth and swallowed with the hope that it will certainly not kill her but surely kill the prestige and reputation of Nilay sir and his bright mission. Having consumed rat poison, I was the first person to whom she had informed. Heavens fell upon me no sooner. I heard the news. I rushed rapidly towards sir's home. She was already in the hospital before I reach. Somebody had told the news Nilay sir who was surveying his distant college of Champawati district. The news fell on him like a thunderbolt. He brust into profusely weeping aloud, repent with sorrowful clamour. He requested his car driver to make him reach the hospital immediately. Several times, his heart throbbed to break and breath disappeared. He died many hundred times on the way, while reaching the hospital.

39

The Hospital Scene

The scene of hospital was very pitiable and woeful. Sir was crying with heart-rendering shriek like an insensible boy. Sometimes, he panted, gasped several times when he laid on the ground. He put his holy and great forehead on the feet of attending doctors and aids. His eyes were red, bloody tears were unceasingly dropping his mouth was automatically dry. Sometimes, he appeared speechless like a mad dog. He was running here and there. He implored with every person whosoever reached. He was so badly shocked that he had certainly died unless the doctors have not consoled him.

When I reached the emergency room of the district hospital, I was terribly shocked and stunned to see the physical condition and lamentation of Nilay sir, though the condition of Anala Ma'm was out of risk. The doctors had announced that there was nothing to worry about her life. The medical officers justified that she had taken a very little amount of rat poison. They were mocking that her act was more to threaten than to die. But Nilay sir was quiet ignorant about this mysterious foul act under the heavy load of repentance, sorrow and realisation of self-guilt. He was trembling like a *peepal* leaf. In the mean time, Anala Ma'm made a loud shriek like an avalanche fell on him.

Sir fell on the ground and began to roll and writhe. The news spread among sir's relatives and friends like a forest fire. Many people had gathered. Sir was completely insane. He was continuously mourning and slobbering. One of his journalist friends pursuaded him not to make such clamour, otherwise the government agencies and police will accuse him for making his wife to take poison. Under subdued breath, sir said, "Let everybody know and hear about it, I don't care for myself but I want to save her life at any cost. O! God what reply will I make to my sole self, to society, friends and relatives?. I will not face my children, my ruin is certain, whether the law punishes me or God, but I do not let leave any stone unturned to bring my wife back in my life."

It was impossible for me to bear this pathetic condition and visage of Nilay sir. I was myself dying with fear and sorrow. Many people were ridiculing and proving sir's act another drama. A few were very sorry on sir's humble lot and those who were good and genial as well-wishers, were shedding tears. invoking upon several deities, I was imploring and seeking to release sir from this agonising melodrama. In this misearable time, one statement of Socrates flashed around my mind. I began to see the thundering voice of Dr. Nilay sir in my mind as he would often convince me whenever any predicament befell on me "O! Tulsi, don't weep, don't be sad, don't think about evils 'No evil can happen with a good man either in life or after death." I was awakened from this day-dream by the words of someone else saying "Analawati Ma'm has opened her eyes. She is looking at us and asking about her children." I rushed into the emergency room, my heart beat became somewhat normal to see whether she was well. The main doctor, who was handling her case announced, "She is quite well now, out of danger. If you want, let her stay tonight in the hospital. She can go early in the morning. I had discharged her by prescribing some precautionary medicine. The glucose drips will continue over night to maintain her power and energy."

I felt enormous peace and satisfaction. Sir was now silent and serious. The shedded furrows of tears were visible on his face into his galled eyes like the lines on a map. We were thanking God for his mercy and extraordinary benevolence. But the joy was momentary perhaps. Almighty providence has incarnated Dr. Nilay sir, as the best example of Hardian philosophy the unique fatalist of Victorian era that "Happiness is but an occasional episode in general drama of pain."

PART–V

40

Scene of Horrible Violence

No sooner did Nilay sir get solace than the gang of disturbing ruffians reached there. They thronged over the whole emergency ward like the swarm of locusts. Most of them were drunk and moody. They were making lot of noise. An elderly person out of them spoke aloud in his native dialect, "Where is Anala? What has happened to her? Who has caused this? O! God they have killed my daughter. They have killed my heifer. I will not leave any person of Nilayawa's family alive. I will kill them without ado. It is their conspiracy. They have altogether forced my daughter commit suicide".

Shouting aloud at each others', they started fighting and quarreling ferociously whosoever come before them. Within few moments, the whole emergency ward of the district hospital changed into a conflicting bout. Nearly all the family members of Nilay sir's side including women were beaten and thrashed badly. They were creating an uproar with filthy abuses. I was shockingly afraid to see their *tandav*. Hardly, I have escaped myself from their seize, under confusion and panic, I rushed out of the hospital. Being aloof from the hospital room of Analwati, I felt relaxed as I was standing in a complete darkness. There was no fear of being fallen in this murky dispute. From there,

I was watching and listening everything being invisible like Tiresius of the waste land. It was no use to enquire about them. Their language, words and clamour proved they were hooligans of Dr. Nilay sir's in-law house, including father-in-law, mother-in-law, brothers-in-law ruffian friends and relatives. It was quiet evident with their haughty aggresive behaviour, bad temperament, ferocious words, obscene and vulgar abuses that they did not have any love or respect for Nilay sir and his family. Everybody knew well that they were not real in relation and affection rather they had a lot of prejudice with his towering prosperity and fame. They were always searching for such opportunities to attack vehemently at the honour and reputation of Nilay sir.

The root cause of their envy was, sir's few months before dismissal as they were working in sir's institution and due to their bad nature and character, they were removed altogether off. At the time of dismissal, they confronted very bitterly, sir had replied vice-versa. So, they had left his institution, threatening him of fatal consequences. The fate was working against and adversely to Nilay sir. It provided an opportunity to them. Those ruffians were so rude and out of sense that they did not spare even the veiled women. The wife of Nilay sir's eldest brother who was quiet innocent, meek and humble, the drunken goondas pulled her hand and slapped her nose, called her with several ugly names. His brothers got badly injured. They were abusing and beating everybody as well as crying hypocritiealy shedding crocodile tears. I could not remain there, I neared the room and stood among strangers to see whether this drama of daughterly love by her step mother and brothers in real.

41

Unlike the In-laws

Events rolled on before my eyes. Like Tiresius throbbing between two lives of Nilay Sir and Anala, I was gazing everything silently.

My mind was hammering. I was making several questions to myself "Are father-in-law and mother-in-law like such as they are? Is it called the love and honour of relatives? Are relatives like this? Are there such mean men in the world who marry their daughters with a person whose demolish and insult keeps no value for them?."

Everything was going on in the verandah outward. The emergency hall of the hospital was mute. Nilay sir who was into the emergency room, beside the headpost, Analwati Devi did not see anything happened outside. Only some grieved and awe provoking news reached him by some faithful teachers of Nilay sir who have accompanied him. I thanked God many thousand times for his invaluable bounty of providing Nilay sir with faithful staff members and friends. How can I forget to Shamsad Ahmad, Praveen Tiwari and Kamal Srivastava sir, the seniormost teachers of Nilay sir, who were not only perfect teacher, but were ever helpful in supporting and cooperating friends of Nilay sir. How can I forget the name and face of Vimal Chandra Sharma, the old and elderly', perhaps the most devoted friend who proved his friendship like twenty four carrot pure gold, during misery. The lanky grave and wise person in white, leaderly dresses with a power spectacle on nose, aging nearly fifty five, Vimal Chandra Sharma remained fixed nearly for more than thirty six hours with Dr. Nilay sir in the hospital. He chased Nilay sir very quickly wherever he went, taking several opinions and advices here and there. He was blaming, comforting and supporting Nilay sir in the most critical hours. He was perhaps extremely shocked and sorrowful to see the hovering risks and dangers on Nilay sir's head. So, he was not ready to leave him alone for a single moment. God knows why they left sir physically unharmed, while they pulled him several times for the counter talk in a very hateful tone. The father-in-law of Nilay sir Jagga and sir's eldest brother-in-law Hayagreev asked him "O! Sharma tell me, how much wrong had they done with my daughter. Suppose, what would you do if someone treated your daughter so badly? I will not let Nilay, the debauchee go without punishment. We will not leave him by abuses and insults, but beat him half-dead, if he dies, let it be."

Standing motionlessly, unshakingly with fixed gesture Vimal Chandra Sharma sir was standing speechlessly without comment. Although, Vimal Chandra Shrama was a local inhabitant of nearby colony of the district hospital, who had many friends, brothers, relatives, supporters and nephews, but he was also helpless. He could do nothing to stop this obscene conflict. The quarrel did certainly continue for a while, if an accidental patient with hundreds of men with district officers and police had not reached the spot. Suddenly, the atmosphere got changed. The flourishing goondas fled and peace returned in madam Analawati's ward. She had quiet been well now. She was talking with care takers. I thanked God again with my heart deep passions, as the filthy battle was not witnessed by Dr. Nilay sir. Neither many people could know what the vulgur dispute was all about. A very soul-searching question was clouding in my mind which was bursting my heart. It was why they had left Nilay sir without insulting perhaps, they were shattered by the officers and policemen and did not find chance to reach him. I had this little satisfaction which it did not demoralise Nilay sir.

Night was passing fastly. The hands of clock had striken five in the dawn. Everybody of Nilay sir's side remained standing overnight. So, their mental and physical fatigue could have easily been guessed. Everybody was contented that the storm was over. A very old woman of Nilay sir's relation pursuaded him. O! son Nilay, don't take it on heart if the life of anybody's daughter be fell in such peril, he will surely make less or more halla balla at the time. But, the tempest was not over in true senses. The misery had not harboured. Hardly our heart beats were normal nearly thirty hours had passed, we were facing the obscene drama of insult and abuse. Now, the atmosphere was little silent.

42

The Elder Step Brother-in-Law

All of a sudden, there was bolt from the blue which broke off the silence of emergency hospital room, early in the morning. Everybody could hardly understand what was happening as a gang of notorious criminals followed by Nilay sir's second brother-in-law named Karata reached there. He was a constable in distant district of other province, an arrogant, proud and boastful man of bad temperament. There remained no peace between Nilay sir and him. He was so wicked that he didn't like to appreciate the virtues of anybody else. Though, he was only an amateur police constable, everybody of his family with father Jagdish Prasad, boasted about him to be a powerful and prestigious police officer like D.I.G. Abusing beastly, the boorish hooligan caught hold Nilay sir in his arm and dragged him out of the room. All the envious members of Karat's family surrounded Nilay sir and the vulgar drama of threatening and blackmailing started there in full swing. Addressing to the public in emotion mass, Karat the cursed and venomous snake of Jagga's family began to spill out his poison to parch Nilay sir's reputation. He proclaimed—O! People of Brahmapuri, look at this man standing here. You know everybody appealing to him. You all honour him, regarding as a best teacher and a greatman,

. but you don't know how mean, depraved, and dirty person he is. He is a big immoral rogue, a debauchee, a fraud and a man of badly loose character. Come! Come everybody, see! And welcome him I am unmasking his face to make you see about his realiy. O! brother, inform the city inspector of police station to register an F.I.R. I will make him taste the jail wind even today O! brothers, call the media persons, so that they may picture this lust-devotee on their front page or as a breaking news. O! God, he has crossed the limits of immorality and lustfulness, keeps many women flirt and visits several houses in the night. Don't send your sisters and daughters to his institutions to study, otherwise he will seduce them. He has tortured and troubled my sister so badly that she has committed suicide. It was our attempt and God's wish that she was saved. We will beat him dead today here that will not be enough to avage on his offence. This short fat glutton gobbles up the cooked food and leaves no part for his children and wife. This lusty man perhaps gives this very lesson to his followers."

Sir was standing rather silent with his faithful staff members. His everlasting friend Vimal Chandra Sharma was there. The scene of infamy and insult was so foul and horrible that none can describe in terms. I have seen many quarrels, disputes and controversies in reality and in fiction, but I have never seen any kinsman of anybody else behaving so filthily breaking the boudaries of insult, abuse and blasphemy. Nilay sir would often tell me about the bad behaviour of his law house members but today I had been the eyewitness. I deeply realised that in their minds particularly in Karat's brain, there was not a bit of honour touched for his venerable brother-in-law, who was the guide of many staggering feet in Brahmapuri.

The episode of threat, blackmail and insult with foul abuses did not stop. Karat was filled with malice that it demoralised the whole atmosphere. Avoiding the people's eyes, I was staring at sir's face with stealithy eyes. Now, he was standing as accredited saint rapt in the meditation of God. He wiped hurriedly the sudden drops of tears coming spontaneously from his thoughtful gentle eyes. Nilay sir neither spoke nor opposed nor commented at their heinous charges. Composing my both hands, I was earnestly praying Lord Shiva to whom sir worshipped genuinely "Hey! Maha Dev, "you are omniscient i.e., knows everything, nothing is hidden in your eyes. Save this gentle guide of humanity out of this obscene whirlpool, give him patience enough to bear this burnt and support his heart to supply healthy blood through his coronary arteries so that they may not be blocked with tragic passion." Certainly, it was Nilay sir who could bear such terrible insult and mental suffering as providence has filled him with profound patience. Karat, the filthy and boorish man of boastfulness got suffocated and exhaustedly nervous, while abusing Nilay sir vulgarly, but it did not affect Nilaly sir too much. A quote from the *'Ramayana'* passed through my brain as when the *'Ravana'* the ten-headed devil abused and insulted Lord *Rama* in the presence of *Hanuman* after being released from the Brahmaphans *Hanuman* had only said this—

"Prabhu ko jo adham

Kaha tumne

Isse kab mahima ghatti hai

Kitna bhi phenko dhool kintu

Suraj tak nahi pahunchti hai."

And two lines more—

"Kshad bhar tak bhi

In baton ka

Unpar to nahin prabhav raha
Wah Nirmal Nishkalank Sevak
Waise hi saral swabhav raha."

"No evil can happen with a good man
either in life or after death."

It has well been said by the seers and prophets of the bygone era but I have found the true and living example nearly three long hours have passed. The audience of Karat's vulgar speeches have got badly tired, but his abuses and disgusted insults found no end. His abuses made the common people grieved and angry. Everybody was willing for his silence, but Karat accompanied with his father and brothers did not seem silent. A kin, perhaps the elder brother-in-law [*The Sadu ji*] of Nilay sir's younger brother's law side grew furious very much. He protested strongly and perhaps taught them nice lessons if Nilay sir would not have interrupted politely, but only few words of protest worked much as many people supported him in this attack. Now, seeing the wrathful brows of the mob, Karat accompanied with his father Jagdish Prasad and eldest brother, stopped abusing and left the hospital building, threatening Nilay sir to see him legally in the future. With his departure, the whole hospital atmosphere turnd peaceful. No doubt, the storm has passed over, but its turbulance was still present in my brain.

43

Discharge From the Hospital

The state of our perturbed mind was alarmed again at the call of senior physician, who was attending to Anala ma'm. Nilay entered the hospital room to see whether the doctor listen to his opinion. Addressing Nilay sir, the senior physician said, "Hark,! Mr. Mourner, I haven't seen anybody else so grieved and agonised as you were in the last several hours by appearance. I believe you to be a sane and sound person, but inwardly you are weak and poor. You have made a lot of lamenting that has infected me so badly that I can never forget you. Your genuine passion and affection has expressed the riskful suffering of your wife. Now, she is quite well. You take her home. She must avoid heavy drugs nearly for six months. We all were extremely happy listenning to the physician proclaimation without making any delay. Dr. Nilay sir hired a taxi and returned home with satisfied look.

44

The Self-Condemnation

After the hospital episode, the life and action of Nilay sir got nearly suspended. Everything appear stopped, but the time was running at its natural pace. The days were passing away fast. A week passed unaccountedly and the first Sunday the day of rest and holiday came after the event. Dr. Nilay sir was staying at home in those days. All of a sudden, I couldn't know; neither anybody told me who triggered the atmosphere that commemorised the pungent behaviour of Jagga and Karat. The peace at home was broken again badly as Dr. Nilay sir began to lament and cry with full-throated voice. He was mourning so poignantly and loudly that gathered the *Mohalla* dwellers. Everybody was pursuading and requesting sir to stop weeping, but the efforts were of no use. Weeping profusely, he was only asking everyone, "O! My neighbourhood brothers, sisters aunts and uncles, tell me whether I am a debauchee, speak, immediately do I have loose character? Am, I a devil of society?' With that Nilay sir, again started lamenting loudly. Everybody from neighbourhood pursuaded sir that he had never been such. Everybody was stunned why Nilay sir was asking such questions. An elderly woman opposite his house to whom Nilay sir considered as mother and kept this relation, could not remain silent, she began to weep and cry aloud saying that "Who is the devil to call you a debauchee O! my son, I have been living here for twenty years with you. I have always marked that you never look at any girl or lady of the whole *mohalla.* I can take oath several times for your purity and chastity. May the fire catch their tongues, who is blaming you with such unjust charges. Don't weep and grieve, omniscient "Allah pak" knows everything. He will punish them all, O! My son you are the guide, leader and guardian of several confused pedestrians. If you weep so heartlessly what will happen to them."

For hours, Nilay sir remained lying silent on a wooden plank. The crowd dispersed one by one. "I, Tulsi the most unfortunate lady officer of Nilay sir's institutions had been the eyewitness of the mental anguish, confessional laments and sir's innocent repentance, but I could do nothing to stop such disasters.

45

The Villainy

Time is the most powerful force in itself. Nothing can check its mighty footsteps. It runs on spontaneously. It had been the eyewitness of several emperors and kings rise and downfall as *Mandhata* the ornament of *Satyuga;*. Augustus the glory of Rome and Alexander the great, the world conqueror of Greece.; Time paves path for new dreams and hopes. It can heal up the bigger injury. It had also made sir's mind and temperament somewhat fresh, balanced and healed. Once again, the Ulysses of Brahmapuri started on his glorious mission of educating the world and its strugglers. He attempted his best to re-establish his honour, prestige and happiness forgetting his past, but destiny was against him. Perhaps, she was not happy in his delight. After departing from the hospital, Nilay sir's father-in-law Jagdish Prasad (Jagga) and his brother-in-law Karat, a *gunda* by nature and temperament, though he always wore on the garb of a gentle police constable, began to spread several scandalous rumours among Nilay sir's relatives, friends, guardians and well-wishers. As I have previously said, the time was against Nilay sir, consequently everybody believed in Jagga's narration. The scandal that Nilay sir had nearly killed his wife by poisoning due to the company of several lascivious women created an atmosphere of hate and insult throughout his institutions. The scandalous rumour played havoc as many persons began to spit in the name of Nilay sir. A cousin-brother from Nilay sir's father's sister side came to discuss about his ignoble and infamy matter, Nilay sir was stunned to listen to his questioning. During the course of verbal discourse, it was revealed that it was the foulest attempt of Jagga and Karat to destroy his reputation as a whole. It angered Nilay sir very much. He went to Jagga to discuss about his act of rumours. A fierce war of words took place among sir, Jagga and Karat. Both of them challenged one another to see each other according their own ways.

Jagdish Prasad and Karat had pre-planned for bringing Nilay sir's downfall, as they had collected the photocopies of every medical reports, hospitalised records and patient's description during Anala's act of taking rat poison. They lodged police complaint against Nilay sir, describing the whole story of Anala's poison taking with heavy charges of woman torture, exploitation, beating, bloodshed with more sugar and spice. Some recent cases of women's rape and killing had created turmoil in the whole country several women at the time defending bills which has recently passed by the parliament.

46

The Arrest of Nilay Sir

Fate worked again fatally for Dr. Nilay sir as the women related crimes were being discussed across India. In the very time, sir was accused with such allegations the inspector of city police station handled this case very seriously. With his police team, the inspector Randhir Singh reached the residence of Nilay sir in the wee hours at his head office. The inspector informed the security guard of his main gate to call Nilay sir for parley. The guard was badly surprised to see the police team on the gate, calling Nilay sir after his name. Dr. Nilay, a well routined person was taking some rounds of his green campus during morning stroll. Without waiting, the police inspector reached sir, following the guard and arrested him announcing several serious charges on him on behalf of his father and brother-in-law Jagdish Prasad and Karat. Sir was stunned to see this uninformed and unexpected police raid into his head institution, which he considered holier than a shrine. Sir tried to say something, but Randhir Singh the aggressive police inspector did not listen to any excuses. They did not let him change the track suit and took him to the jail without any hue and cry.

49

Solitary Confinement

47

Solitary Confinement

The news of sir's arrest spread across the city like forest fire. A great number of people began to collect daily outside the district jail to see him. I "Tulsi", the fateless viewer of everything reached jail to meet and see Nilay sir, throbbing between two lives of split-consciousness. Having completed the formalities of the jail manuals, I reached the closet of Nilay sir. Everybody began to gaze at me as I burst aloud weeping to see his hard solitary confinement. Only few days of captivity have changed sir completely. Like a caged animal, he was running here and there. His face was blown and sapped out. He was looking unfixedly. His shirt was unbuttoned. He began to mourn noticing me weeping. My whole body was shuddering badly. My senses felt numbed. I was about to fall down on the ground. So, I could not face him for a long. I returned home, sobbing and sighing heavily.

PART–VI

48

Trial in the Court

The next day was the day of sir's trial in the court. His case was being heard in a fast track court on the very day. He was questioned very harshily by the cunning lawyer of Jagdish Prasad's side. The lawyer said to sir, "Are you the owner of several schools and colleges?" Sir said "Yes". Are you also a teacher and a preacher and a moral lecturer of your institution?" Sir again shook his head in affirmative. The lawyer further asked "Do you treat your wife very badly and make a lot of quarrel and fighting with her?" sir again said "Yes". "Do you have illegal and immoral relations with several women?" Sir said "God knows"; "Do you have a very foul and loose character?" sir again repeated "God knows" without, any further delay or discussion an old judge, the saviour of moral humanity and securer of holy chastity announced his judgment.

"As the situation describes, Dr. Nilay being a teacher, founder and manager of several educational institutions committed heinous crimes of exploiting his wife, subjecting her to domestic violence and woman torture. So, he is subjected to punishment under the section of 498A Indian Penal Code 376." "He is sentenced three year-long solitary confinement with a fine of Rs. 10,000. If he fail to pay the fine, he shall suffer six months more under captivation as his case comes in the rim of rare cases, where a teacher, a moral guide of society commits such grave offences in his veiled life which none could apprehend. His innocent wife has suffered everything mutely. She never tried to inform any legal authorities about the injustices on her. The court pays a lot of compliment to Jagdish Prasad i.e., Jagga Ji as well as Karat, the dutiful police constable, who have brought this sin into the light of the court".

Throughout the trial and order, I remained there listening very carefully the plea of the lawyers and magistrate. One thing that affected some audience in the court as well as to me, was mute acceptance of levelled charges by Nilay sir without any protest or opposition. It was completely expressing paradox to Jagga's allegations felt by some, but none protested.

Two policemen immediately reached there and took Nilay sir back to jail. I continued watching this irony of life, while sir went away with his bent head and downcast eyes, the poor man was truly helpless.

49

Release on Bail

The absence of Nilay sir played havoc over his institutions. Everything was looking insignificant, dry, insipid and tasteless. The morning assembly which would always filled us into a new life and energy turned futile. Everything seemed stopped. I was very anxiously waiting for Nilay sir's release from jail, but the time was waiting for none. It was continuously running on its usual speed. Six months have rolled away – I continued discussing with Vimal Chandra Sharma on phone about the progress in legal preparation for releasing Nilay sir, when his answers and expressions did not satisfy me, I directly went to Sharma Ji and asked about the process of his release Vimal Chandra Sharma said, "I am myself badly upset with Nilay sir's absence, "Tulsi, things have been in disorder. Several employees of the institution are not following the rules and discipline. Well, I am doing my best to bring Nilay sir out of the jail. Today I have asked very earnestly to the lawyer Ateequllah Khan, who is also Nilay sir's best friend. He had assured me to release sir this evening.

Ateequallah Khan, a learned lawyer of criminal law filled a bail suit, giving strong grounds for gaining release of Nilay sir, on bail in his proceeding he said, "Your majesty, Dr. Nilay to whom the court has given three years of servitude is a thorough going gentleman, a friend of humanity and good to every section of human societies. His absence among the common man is doing an irreparable national loss, as he is the gardener of national nursery, whose nourishment has been providing several future pillars of the nation for many years, I do not know the situation, which has forced him commit any wrong, but one thing I know is that, if he is not released, it shall perish the life and future of several hundreds of youth, altogether." Having heard such truthful plea of Ateequllah Khan, the defence counsellor of Dr. Nilay sir, the honourable judge of the court allowed Dr. Nilay sir's release immediate on bail.

Several faithful persons accompanied with more than hundred obedient students, were already waiting on the main gate of the district jail. They were in the mood of making loud applause, but Nilay sir beekoned them to remain silent. The crowed followed him till his home in silence. On reaching home, Nilay sir mutely went into his bedroom and slept without speaking any word.

50

Conditions to Compromise

As I was living in the same house of Nilay sir's first floor, I slept peacefully. Early in the morning, some pitiable voice awakened me. I began to peep through the iron grill in the ceiling of courtyard. The scene which I witnessed was really pathetic. Composing his both hands, Nilay sir was imploring Anala, pursuading her not to create any disturbance futher, as he is ready to compromise with her, under her pre-set conditions. Anala said, "Ok, now listen! My demands and conditions.I am numbering one by one—

1. You shall give Rs. 25,000 per month to me for my personal expenditures without any question.
2. You shall not appoint any lady staff for your personal support.
3. No administration shall be handled by any lady.
4. You shall neither play nor laugh nor visit by any party on feast or banquet with any woman folk.
5. Neither any woman nor you exchange any gift or prize on any occasion.
6. You shall not make any photo shoot with any lady or girl.

7. None shall celebrate your birthday.
8. None shall admire particularly your personality and attire.
9. You shall not do anything without my permission.
10. You shall love and admire those persons whom I love and admire.

Nilay sir accepted all conditions mutely without protest or objection. Having compromised the way with madam Analawati Devi, sir took a deep breath of satisfaction, came out of his bedroom, got ready, and turned out for work putting his black shining coat on his right shoulder hanging. Throughout the day, he remained strolling here and there in the green play ground of his institution, as if he were meditating upon some serious issue.

51

Attempt for Re-Inhabitation

Days were spending fast. There was no change in the behaviour of Nilay sir's daily routine. He would come to the college during assembly time and remained walking throughout the day in the school playground. Nearly everything was running normally except some whispers of evil natured ladies regarding his imprisonment. Nothing was abnormal, six months went off. One day, Nilay sir called his employees including teaching staff, office staff, travel and security staff altogether. Everybody was thinking differently about this meet. Actually, the administrative personnel of his institute were thinking that sir would certainly ask about the speed of progress about present and future condition. But when sir opened his heart, everybody was surprised that Nilay sir was not making any inquiry about any branch of his educational institution, rather he was proposing something else. Addressing the staff members of his institutions, sir said, "My dear teachers! And faithful members of my Saint Vivekanand group of educational institutions, listen! peacefully! "We are all living in a very progressive and regressive era, as we achieved fast development in the materialistic fields, contrarily we have destroyed much of our spiritual wealth. We work hard, why? Certainly, for money and what is the use of money? Certainly, for bringing the joys of the home, but simultaneously we forget the joys out of materialistic gain without spiritual uplift. In true sense, we have achieved nothing, because we have no achievement in the field of humanity, charity and spirituality. Concluding my speech, I want to say," Let us do something which can bring a flick of smile on those faces, who are lying buried under the heavy load of poverty, illiteracy, misery and helplessness. Plainly, I mean to say may we not give a very little amount of our earning in purchasing the joys of those poor children, who have no clothes to wear even in such coldest winter? Actually, I am going to organise a civil society under the title *'Nirbalo Uddhar Samiti'* to help the poor and downtrodden of our country." Everybody was ready to help and support Nilay sir in his noble mission. The names were registered and the dates were fixed for the monthly meeting of *Nirbalo Uddhar Samiti.*

After the departure of persons I drowned into the sea of thought. I was overwhelmed to see the liveliness of Nilay sir during his liberal speeches of morality and spirituality, but the fate was working against sir, perhaps she did not like the joys, happiness and divine smile of Nilay sir who sent Vikram a wicked ill-natured and a chronic foe of Nilay sir in the meeting of *Nirbalo Uddhar Samiti'*. It was the time of Sunday midday perhaps the third meeting of *Nirbalo Uddhar samiti* was arranged in the uppermost conference hall of Nilay sir's first school building. One by one, several members and post-holders of samiti have addressed the assembly. Nilay sir was extremely happy and content, as he was a magician to get victory over his depressing thoughts. He was forgetting his bitter past very fast. Today, he was addressing the crowd with renewed energy, extreme vigour and excellent will-power. Addressing the people, he said, "We must swear to commit the following:

1. We shall donate the 100th part of our annual income every year.

2. We shall honour every religion.
3. We shall try to speak the truth.
4. We will try to amend the corrupt and wicked person.
5. We will not allow anybody else let injustice on our society so forth.

PART–VII

52

The Pungent Comment

All the people supported sir's views. Nearly everybody admired Nilay sir's wisdom and common sense. When the meeting was through, a man named Vikram lifted his hand and spoke, "I want to say something." Dr. Nilay, who was the president of the committee as well as presiding over the meeting, allowed Vikram speak freely. Vikram was a great opponent of Nilay sir, who always delighted in sir's anguish and tears. Sir had done nothing wrong on him except some opposition concerning his lawless and immoral deeds. Any poet has truly said—

"Samaj mein kuchh

Aise darindey hote hain

Chaman mein beej

Jo hans kar zahar ka bote hain"

No doubt, Vikram was the ugly satan of the society, who vomitted forth venom when he spoke. He said, "First of all, any man must amend and improve oneself before improving others Nilay sir. You need more amendment about your conduct, character and behaviour, particularly with your wife who is a sole victim of your tyranny. A man like you has no moral right to speak like a saint and address such committees as you have been doing." Vikram was the close neighbour of Nilay sir, a postman of bad rumours and scandals from outward to ma'm Analawati. Whenever Madam Anala found chance, she always narrated foul about sir's character and behaviour to Vikram and his wife. With the expression of these words, Vikram vanished, but everybody was stunned listenning him.

The meeting dispersed with whispering and low communication about Nilay sir's whereabout, for others it was a trivial matter, but it was a big cause of thinking for Nilay sir. The event humiliated him terribly. He was suffering badly from the sense of self-guilt realisation overnight he could not sleep peacefully. Many times, he sat up while awaking ultimately he said to himself Vikram was right. I have no right to teach others about the lessons of goodness, morality and nobility. After much repenting, Nilay sir dismissed the promise of holding prime responsibilities of the civil society, and he broke off the very society.

53

The Law-Camp

Time was passing off at normal speed. Chance and coincidences were playing their damaging role in woeful journey of Nilay sir. One day, it so happened that something maddened Nilay sir. He remained restless and unrelaxed after civil society's meeting. Now, he was attempting to be normal. In the meantime, there appeared a heavy thunderbolt from the blue.

The judiciary of the district headquarter, particularly the district judge selected sir's first educational campus for sponsoring a law camp. Actually, it was the instruction from the higher authorities to the District Judge to go among the children and tell them about their legal rights. They must be told about the law against their exploitation and harassment.

54

The Appalling Effect

Although, the camp had been arranged for telling the children about their legal rights, some ladies out of college staff kept some villainy, perhaps for Nilay sir's life and family, exhibited some hand made paintings revealing the cruelty of honour killing and domestic violence. God knows, what occurred in their minds. They demonstrated a very horrible scene of domestic violence wherein stout muscular man was clutching tightly the plait of a fragile woman in one hand and a thick stick in another hand with cruel and fiery eyebrow while the woman was looking very pitiable as her head was bleeding and big drops of tears were vividly painted on her mourning face. The organiser of the school teaching staff had planted the painting on the very front of the elevated platform near the stage during the law camp. There was a remark on the painting "Stop!!! Domestic violence."

The painting made a mind-blowing effect upon Nilay sir, I like 'Tiresius' though worldly blind knew no more about the outer cunning world, was throbbing between two lives of Anala and Nilay, could do nothing to stop his melancholy, but only as a dumb spectator was looking the 'Eliot's' Wasteland helplessly.

I noticed at once that something was badly troubling Nilay sir. He stood up and sat again, looking unfixedly here and there as if something aching or paining him or he had recieved any bad news or he wanted to go out of the camp. As the law camp was only a formality, none came to know about his restlessness.

Sir's strange ups and downs were disturbing the harmony of legal lectures, being delivered by law delegates. Anyway, I waited till those judges, barristers and advocates went away. No sooner did they go than I asked Nilay sir, "What has happened with you sir? Why were you behaving abnormally? Has something gone wrong with you? Do you have any pain or trouble?" I posed these questions. Sir did not answer. Actually, he was still not in normal mood. I shook his shoulders saying, SssssissssRsss? My shake brought him back to senses, raising a finger at the painting of domestic violence sir said, "O! Tulsi look at this picture. It is appalling me." It has shaken my whole being badly, "Tulsi" Why they had painted my picture on the place of cruel man ?" "I am not so, Tulsi" call forth those teachers, who have made this prepared" I was taken aback to listen his calamity, but laughed declaring that there was no feature of his face in the painting. How sir had taken it to have resembled him. I began to convince and assure very politely and dearly. "O! sir your face has not been painted. Not a single feature simulate with it." O! Please don't panic me. I am myself dying with fever and headache for last two days. Don't frighten me any more" Sir came into himself, putting his turned fingers on my forehead, he said, "O! Child, you have truly high fever. Go to the physician and treat yourself well. You may take my monetary help." Wiping my tears with my right hand, I descended down from the uppermost conference hall and got mixed with common people of the court.

PART–VIII

55

A Visit to Psychiatrist

Many weeks were spent without any uncommon occurence, but the painting exhibition did not disappear completely from my mind, even after nearly two months. I was again and again thinking about it. Ultimately, I visited a psychiatrist and narrated the whole story, telling everything about sir's background and conjugal life.

The psychiatric listened very carefully what I said, at last he said. "There is no need to be worried any more about your sir's sanity or mental health. One thing is quite evident from your discourse that he is too thoughtful person. "Madam" we general human beings cannot understand the validity, depth, power and spread of human mind. Shakespeare was quiet justified when he has said," 'A sharp poetic mind can see more devils and witches anywhere than they are present in the vast hell.' Glorifying the unique capability of man's mind, John Milton, the great puritian and sublime poet of metaphysical age has said—

"A mind has its own place
And in itself
Can make a heaven of hell
And hell of heaven."

So, Tulsi!, "It was the density of his thought sphere, which showed your sir's own face in the painting. Perhaps, sir would have thought that maker of the painting regards sir—the similar guiltiful, as they had painted on the canvas and repeated thoughts of sir's mind had vivified his face on the painting. Thus, Dr. Nilay has assumed his image to be on the painting. There is neither any need of medicine nor any particular precaution. You can do one thing for his normal thinking if you can, "Don't leave him alone for hours.Make him laugh and advise him to see comic movies. He needs enjoyment,peace and happiness." I was much thankful to God to know that nothing was abnormal to sir's mind.

56

Attempts of Depression

I returned home and went to madam Analawa to shore the anguish of Nilay sir. I have told her that sir needed happiness and comfort more than anything. She must try to keep him happy. She listened carelessly and jeered at the end. "You and so many people of his empire are caring him. What is my need to do so? He is Ok. It is only his drama anew." Whispering the names of several deities, I ascended into my room leaving everything on God.

For nearly six months, everything remained normal or I might have felt it so.

But one day, I was profoundly shocked to listen the wailful imploring of Nilay sir before his wife. I tried to see in his room, but I could not see anything as the door of his bedroom was tightly shut with stealthier footsteps. I went to the door and began to peep through the slanting. The scene which I saw was awe some again I saw therein Nilay sir, my father, my teacher, my moral guide and my patron in the same miserable condition as I had seen him many times earlier. With blood-red eyes and amid the constant flowing tears, sir was imploring with his composed hands, the content which I heard pieceined was like thus "O! Anu (i.e., Analawati) don't say so she is a very young lady equal to my daughter. I had taught her from very early classes besides she is a young widow, who has already suffered much. Don't try to defame her by creating this new scandalous rumour about her. "O! Dear, Reetu is foolish she does not know how and what should be asked. If she asked about the effect of quarrel on our family it is her big foolery. Please excuse her. She is not sensible enough. She is neither deprived nor she is after me." With such expressions, sir was continuously beseeching, but there was no effect on Anala Ma'm. Perhaps, she had judged well that this fresh scandal was affecting very deeply to Nilay sir. Perhaps, she fully wanted to make him insane.

57

Attempt to Escape Mumbai

I interrupted knowingly calling upon Anala madam I said," Ma'm I want your electric press for ten minutes." My voice subsided the conflict. Anala ma'm came out with a wicked expression on her face and handed me the press.

The day went very deeply disturbing for Nilay sir, as Anala Ma'm called for Reetu a widow college staff and thrashed her and so insulted that the news reached far and wide everywhere in all the institutions of Nilay sir. The same evening, sir again called me in his prime office room and expressed a lot of sorrow at Anala's behavior. He said, "Tulsi what will the people think? Everybody will believe now that I am really a lecherous and loose character debauchee, as I am pursuing several ladies one after another." I tried at my utmost level to convince sir that he is not wrong in any way, but was profoundly upset for the day and did not calm down.

The day settled and I continued thinking about his destiny. Nilay sir was a versatile genius. He could make up stories quickly, compose poems and songs quickly. After a week, one day, I listened to him, discussing with his proctors, principals and caretakers of all institutions. I was shocked to hear that he was intending to leave his native district Brahmapuri for being settled in Mumbai. He wanted to start his career afresh as a scriptwriter of films. Some of us supported him as the faithful staff members wanted to bring a change in sir's mood and mind. When nearly one month got spent and sir did not go to Mumbai, I could not help asking the reason very seriously and sir replied pessimistic, O! Tulsi how should I tell you my helplessness? Anala raised a war at this with me very vulgarly. She asked "Has your belly not satisfied with the women here as you are going Mumbai for the persuit of call-girls there?"

58

Obscene and Immoral Confession

Nilay Sir remained silent for some time, after a pause he said—

"Tulsi", "It is death for me to speak something, what I want to tell at this time, but now I will tell you one more private but obscene problem, which must not be spoken by me in front of you, as I consider you as my daughter. Because, I will live no more now after this confession. So, I want to say something before my death."

No sooner sir spoke I got extremely terrified. I felt maddened with grief. I was going to create a lot of clamour, uproar and cry. Seeing my horrible form, Nilay sir began to smile divinely. Pursuading me, he said, "O! Foolish, I have lied I am not going to die, I am alive and will be alive. I am strictly against suicide. I always preached not to think about this cowardice act of committing suicide then, how can I do so". My tears subsided, I weepingly requested him not to repeat such sentence again any more. Sir agreed with me. I requested him to tell problems which he called obscene. With a long procastination, sir began to speak with bent head, looking fixedly into the earth. "She is calling me a eunuch. She is also threatening me that she will announce among all the people that I am impotent" I spoke nothing as I was sad and ashamed "I do not wish to make any relation with her. O! God I don't know what happens with me when I associate myself with her. I feel no excitement in her company." Said, Nilay sir. I further remained silent. Sir continued, "Physical relations are much more guided by mind. They are the products of sensational brain. I feel no spur nothing out of her bodily attachment sexualise me. Tulsi, I am not impotent. It is the result of her behaviour, which has created a sexual disharmony between her and me. She does not try to understand. She blames me for making illicit physical relation with some other woman, which loosens my body so nervously, but in true senses, it is not so! It is not so." I was a dumb listener, as I did not know anything about nuptial relations with a very ashamed face. Sir went away. He was badly perturbed, perhaps to know what he had told me.

59

An Ode to Dr. Nilay

Despite intellectual, literary, spiritual and learning excellences, sir had some nice hobbies. He was a fine player of football, badminton and kabbadi. He was the ace rifle-shooter. During sport meets, he taught the youngster, how to shoot a rifle or gun safely and properly. He had gained some awards in gun-firing. After the narration of Anala's new allegation of being impotent, sir did not go home. He stayed into the guest room of one of his institutions that night. I was much terrified with his assertion. I also stayed in the institution, hostel room. All of a sudden, I felt the weather got completely changed. Ferocious eastern wind blew big ghost-like clouds began to hover in the sky. They covered the moon, as if they were swallowing the sky. It was monsoon weather, but was fully unbecoming. The lightening was cleaving the sky's chest. Strange dogs were weeping around the college boundaries. Jackals were clammering unnaturally. I was so upset that, I had forgotten my thrust, hunger, even the nature calls. I mounted atop three storeyed school building, which sir called his watch tower; from there I began to watch on Nilay sir when I found him nowhere in the school campus. I cast my eyes far and wide in his search.

Suddenly, I saw him going towards the security room. I descended down quickly to reach, but the wretched Tulsi died alive, as soon as she heard the gun firing twice.

Stormily, I reached into the gun man's room. My heart broke, my eyes were petrified to see him lying dead on the ground blood-stained. I found a chit of paper lying there with the note.

"O Almighty God and my genuine supporter Tulsi!, Forgive me, I am helpless. Nothing could help or believe on me, only this gun."

I swooned at the very gate of the security guard. I do not know how I reached into my room neither knowing what had happened.

After a couple of days, I heard a news from an English newspaper thus, "Nilay, a school, college manager committed suicide in a very mysterious way. Police and the law proved that he was an abnormal, eccentric and a characterless fellow, who tortured his wife very much, no doubt an evil of society good to death he met and became disappeared from the civilised society of men."

"O! God, thou madest this beautiful earth when will it be ready to receive thy saints, How long, O lord How Long!?